CALLWEY

TABLE OF CONTENT

10
FOREWORD
PETRA RESKI **10**
CHRISTINE COUNTESS VON DER PAHLEN **12**

14
VENICE

16
SAN MARCO
RISTORANTE CLUB DEL DOGE **20**
RISTORANTE QUADRI **26**
GIO'S RESTAURANT **32**
OSTERIA DA CARLA **38**
RESTAURANT ANTICO MARTINI **44**
OSTERIA VINO VINO **50**
BISTROT DE VENISE **56**
INSIDER TIPS & INTERESTING FACTS 62

66
CASTELLO
RESTAURANT WILDNER **70**
RISTORANTE LOCAL **76**
TRATTORIA CORTE SCONTA **82**
VERO VENETIAN ROOTS **88**
RISTORANTE AL COVO **92**
OSTERIA ALLE TESTIERE **98**
INSIDER TIPS & INTERESTING FACTS 102

104
SAN POLO
WISTÈRIA **108**
TRATTORIA ANTICHE CARAMPANE **114**
OSTERIA BANCOGIRO **120**
INSIDER TIPS & INTERESTING FACTS 126

128
SANTA CROCE
RISTORANTE GLAM **132**
OSTERIA ZANZE XVI **138**
INSIDER TIPS & INTERESTING FACTS 142

144
CANNAREGIO
IL GIARDINO SEGRETO **148**
VENICE M'ART **154**
INSIDER TIPS & INTERESTING FACTS 162

164
DORSODURO
RISTORANTE LINEADOMBRA **168**
TRATTORIA ANZOLO RAFFAELE **174**
CIP'S CLUB **180**
INSIDER TIPS & INTERESTING FACTS 186

188
LAGOON
RISTORANTE ADRIATICO TERRACE **192**
TRATTORIA AL GATTO NERO **198**
RISTORANTE VENISSA **204**
INSIDER TIPS & INTERESTING FACTS 210

212
SERVICES
BACARI **214**
MADE IN VENICE **222**
LATE NIGHT SECRETS **226**
EXPERIENCES **228**
TOP EVENTS **230**

232
INDEX

240
IMPRINT

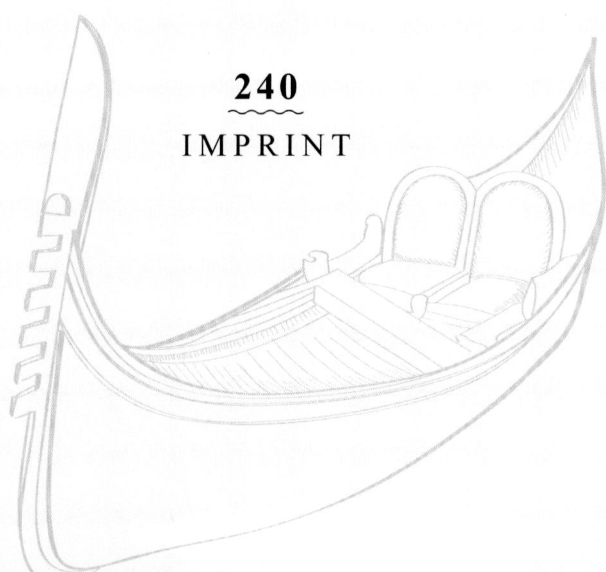

FORE WORD

Every time I say that I live in Venice, I am first met with incredulous looks. And then, with enthusiasm. Ah, so you fell in love with Venice? people usually say. And when I stubbornly reply that I didn't fall in love with Venice, but rather with a Venetian – that Venice, in a way, simply happened to me – they smile indulgently. After all, there are certainly worse fates than colliding with the most beautiful city in the world.

At first, I didn't even see Venice as a real city. It felt more like an illusion. A phantasmagoria. Too beautiful to be true.

I only truly fell in love with Venice when I discovered its vulnerability. When I realized how the city was being mutilated – by the relentless more, more, more of a tourist monoculture that Venetian mayors have been preaching as a kind of state religion for the past thirty years. When Venice was stripped of its essential functions – hospitals closed, islands sold off, schools turned into hotels.

If you're wondering why Venetians keep electing mayors who don't represent their interests: Venice doesn't actually have its own municipal government. Under fascism, the city was forcibly merged with the mainland. And so, when a mayor is elected, it's not the Venetians who choose him, but the residents of the mainland – people whose daily reality is entirely different. One moves on wheels; the other floats on water.

That Venice has fallen into the wrong hands, into the grasp of those who seek to devour it, is merely a passing phase – or so says the Venetian of my life. Unlike me, he doesn't think in decades but in centuries. Venice is modernity itself; he says – provided one understands it correctly. After all, Venice was already a city of sustainability long before the word even existed.

Venice is not lagging behind the present – it is ahead of it. Both as a concrete way of life and as a utopia. Because what else is this city on the water, if not a real-life dreamscape – an impossibility made manifest?

PETRA RESKI

ABOUT PETRA RESKI

Why has she been living in Venice since the 1990s? Because she lost her heart – not just to a Venetian, but also to the most beautiful city in the world, whose fate she deeply cares about. In more than a dozen books, Petra Reski offers profound insights into her life and her fearless fight against corrupt investors, the machinations of the Mafia, and the ruthless sellout of a city loved by people everywhere.

Two reading recommendations: Als ich einmal in den Kanal fiel (The Time I Fell into the Canal), a book about life in Venice, and her latest work, All'italiana!, in which she recounts her attempt to become Italian.

VENETIAN CUISINE

There is no doubt that mass tourism and the supposed expectations of internatio- nal visitors have left their mark on Vene- tian cuisine. On one hand, this has led to hastily prepared tourist menus; on the other, to culinary classics that now ap- pear on fine-dining menus in Rome and Milan as well. One might think this lea- ves little room for authentic, local food.
Fortunately, a closer look reveals that this is not the case. Hidden away from the hustle and bustle, there are still baca- ri – Venice's traditional wine bars – as well as osterie and family-run trattorias that have remained untouched by the changes around them for generations. Though often simpler in presentation, they still offer a rich variety of traditio- nal Venetian dishes, each one deeply connected to the city's history. Over a thousand years ago, Venice's immense wealth was built on its monopoly of rare spices and luxury goods brought from the East: pepper, sugar, saffron, carda- mom, cinnamon, ginger, nutmeg, and, of course, coffee. These coveted products were not only traded lucratively across Europe but also made their way into Ve- netian kitchens, refining the city's cui- sine forever. Beyond its famed seafood and offal dishes, Venice is particularly known for its risottos, which are often paired with fresh vegetables from the la- goon. The ultimate classic? Risi e Bisi – a dish of risotto with sweet peas, pancetta, shallots, Parmesan, and pars- ley. Another favorite is radicchio rosso, a vibrant red lettuce from Treviso, har- vested after the first frost. Among Venice's time-honored dishes is Sarde in Saor, a recipe dating back to the 14th century and even mentioned in Goldoni's plays: sardines marinated in sweet-and- sour vinegar with onions, pine nuts, rai- sins, and spices – a dish originally crea- ted as a long-lasting ration for sailors of the Serenissima. It was these same sailors who brought back the recipe for stockfish from Scandinavia, which has since become a staple of Venetian cui- sine. Bacalà Mantecato – air-dried cod whipped into a creamy spread with olive oil and served on small slices of bread – is still a popular accompaniment to wine. Then as now, the Rialto Market remains the culinary heart of the city. Beyond this iconic marketplace, there are smal- ler fruit and vegetable stands throughout Venice, as well as Sant'Erasmo, often called the city's floating vegetable gar- den. For those who love seafood, ventu- ring beyond the standard offerings is highly recommended. Look out for rare delicacies such as Tartufo di Mare (sea truffles), Capelunghe (razor clams), Moscardini (small octopuses), Canoc- chie (mantis shrimp), and, depending on the season, Moeche – soft-shell crabs that are fried and eaten whole.
When it comes to wine, Venetians have traveled a long road – from the sweet wines of their colonies, to red wines from Dalmatia and white wines from Crete, to favoring regional vineyards in Veneto, Friuli, and the Adige Valley as foreign wines became subject to import duties. In recent years, local winema- king has experienced a revival, particu- larly on the islands of Sant'Erasmo and Mazzorbo, Burano's smaller neighbor. These island vineyards, once abandoned, are now flourishing once more – proof that Venetian traditions, like the city its- elf, are resilient and enduring.

CHRISTINE COUNTESS VON DER PAHLEN

CANNAREGIO
SANTA CROCE
SAN POLO
SAN MARCO
DORSODURO

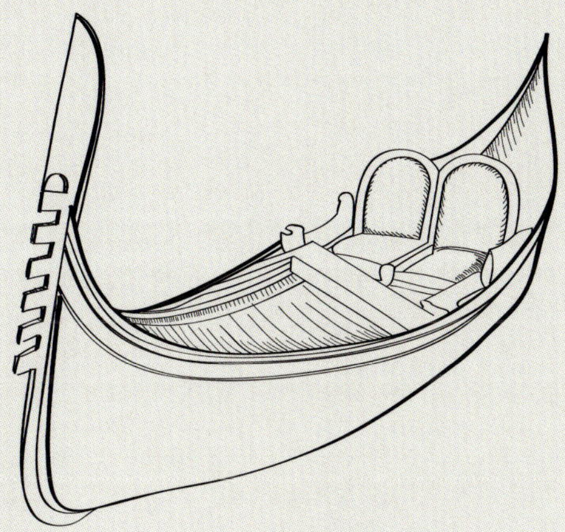

VENICE

Arriving in Venice feels like stepping out of time. Ideally at sunset, one boards a Vaporetto of Line 1 at Santa Lucia station, gliding along the Grand Canal – the world's most famous waterway – straight into the heart of the former maritime republic. Passing 15 churches and around 200 palazzi, their sun-bleached façades rising from the water as silent witnesses of a thousand-year history. Magical, dreamlike, melancholic – almost unreal. On a first visit, one falls head over heels, determined to see and experience everything that makes this floating city so unique – from the bell tower of St. Mark's Basilica to the legendary Harry's Bar. Later, once the initial awe has settled, one begins to embrace the joy of endless wanderings through the labyrinth of narrow alleyways, open to the serendipitous moments waiting around each corner. And eventually, with clearer eyes, one starts to notice the daily life of the fewer than 50,000 remaining Venetians. Yes, despite the nearly 30 million visitors flooding the city each year, local life still exists. It reveals itself in the sestieri – the six districts that structure this book: in San Marco, the former power center of the Serenissima; in Castello, a residential and working-class quarter and home to the Biennale; in Cannaregio, where Europe's first Jewish ghetto was established; in Santa Croce and San Polo, two historic neighborhoods near the Rialto Market; and in Dorsoduro, where gondolas are still repaired to this day. And then there is the lagoon, a centuries-old cultivated water landscape, whose islands serve as summer retreats for both locals and travelers alike.

SAN
MAR
CO

A gondola ride offers an up-close glimpse of hidden canals and secret corners.

The statues on the facade of St. Mark's Basilica symbolize virtues such as wisdom, temperance, and charity.

SAN MARCO

There is no better way to fall in love with Venice than by taking Vaporetto Line 1 from Santa Lucia station to St. Mark's Square. The Grand Canal, Venice's main artery, is at its most breathtaking at sunset when the pastel-colored façades of the nearly contiguous palazzi on either side are bathed in golden light. Arriving at St. Mark's Square, one finds everything that tops the checklist of day-trippers packed into a single space: the Doge's Palace, St. Mark's Basilica, the Campanile, and the arcades of the Procuratie Vecchie and Procuratie Nuove. There is no doubt – this is the very heart of the Serenissima, the square Napoleon once called "the most beautiful drawing room in Europe." For those intent on ticking off every must-see sight, patience is key – much like visiting the Taj Mahal or Hagia Sophia. One absolute highlight is the climb to the top of the Campanile, offering a 360-degree view of a floating paradise – a sea of rooftops and domes awash in saffron, rust, and crimson hues. Returning visitors are usually more relaxed, perhaps even lucky enough to escape the well-trodden tourist paths and discover the quieter charm of small campi – intimate squares lined with churches, noble residences, terrace cafés, and little shops. Seasoned

A panoramic view from the Campanile, the 98.6-meter-high bell tower, is an absolute must.

Newsstands selling newspapers, magazines, souvenirs, and snacks are a Venetian tradition.

Pigeons and seagulls make life especially difficult for visitors on St. Mark's Square.

Ponte Giustinian – one of the many small obstacles for rolling suitcases.

Venice lovers wait until evening before embarking on their long strolls and explorations – never without first enjoying a Spritz or a Prosecco with a breathtaking view from one of the city's many summer terraces.
It's also the perfect time for window shopping along Calle Larga XXII Marzo, where Italian and international luxury brands showcase their coveted goods, including Venice's most exclusive jewelers. For those in search of a peaceful green retreat, the Giardini Ex Reali, reopened in 2019 after five years of restoration, offers a tranquil garden setting with a charming café pavilion. "Venice is a city made for walking," Hemingway once said. That was long ago, but it still holds true today.

Unlike dogs, cats are rarely seen in the city.

At dusk, when the crowds thin out, Venice reveals its former splendor.

RISTORANTE CLUB DEL DOGE

PRIVATE AFFAIR

CLUB DEL DOGE
LOCATED IN THE GRITTI PALACE
SAN MARCO 2467
+39 041-79 46 11
clubdeldoge.com

OPENING HOURS:

Lunch:
Daily from 12:30 PM - 2:30 PM
Dinner:
Daily from 7:00 PM - 10:30 PM
The Gritti Terrace:
Daily from 12:30 PM - 5:30 PM
Bar Longhi:
Daily from 11:00 AM - 1:00 AM

Since the former residence of Doge Andrea Gritti was transformed into a luxury hotel in 1948, The Gritti Palace has been considered the city's finest address, with Club del Doge as its culinary crown jewel. The name itself says it all. It evokes the intimacy of a club where like-minded people find a second home – guests who appreciate being welcomed by name, where personal preferences are carefully noted and honored. And why Doge? What could be more elegant than dining in the former residence of Andrea Gritti, a true Venetian showpiece situated in a prime location on the banks of the Grand Canal? But that doesn't mean strict formalities dominate the experience. At lunch, Club del Doge exudes a relaxed, informal atmosphere. Large communal tables encourage a convivial food-sharing culture. Only in the evening, as the setting sun bathes the surrounding palazzi in golden light, does the restaurant fully embrace its glamorous gourmet identity – with sparkling crystal, classic Blue China, floral centerpieces, and candlelit white linen tables. When General Manager Paolo Lorenzoni, who has been at the helm since 2013, asked loyal guests what they would change, their response was unanimous: as little as possible. And so, during the hotel's most recent renovation, every effort was made to preserve its unique atmosphere while enhancing its beauty and comfort. Today, The Gritti Palace is even more splendid, yet remains true to itself.

It was also Lorenzoni who transformed the previously unused fourth-floor terrace into one of Venice's most coveted new spots. When the weather is fine, Club del Doge guests now gather there for a scenic lunch. At both lunch and dinner, they are in the expert hands of Executive Chef Alberto Fol. Born in Treviso, Fol honed his skills in some of Italy's most prestigious kitchens, including as Executive Chef at the iconic Hotel des Bains in Venice and, most recently, at the Danieli Terrace Restaurant. His signature dishes include: Spaghettone "Senatore Cappelli" with garlic, olive oil, chili, squid, and a touch of blue cheese or Scallops in "Cacciatore Style" Sauce with polenta and mountain herbs. And of course, The Gritti Tiramisu – a must-try classic.

For those who wish to witness Chef Alberto Fol in action, a cooking class at the Gritti Epicurean School is an unforgettable experience.

Wine lovers can opt for a wine tasting curated by Head Sommelier Sandro Chinellato, while those in search of the perfect Martini will be spoiled for choice with the Martini Trolley at Bar Longhi. On warm summer nights, guests can savor their final, blissful moments of the day with a cocktail on one of the two terraces, overlooking the shimmering canal.

Left – The Club del Doge's latest facelift was graced with luxurious Rubelli fabrics and wallpaper.

Below – Executive Chef Alberto Fol, dedicated advocate of modern Venetian cuisine.

RISOTTO "ALLA HEMINGWAY" – A DISH WITH A STORY

RISOTTO À LA HEMINGWAY – A TRIBUTE TO THE LEGENDARY WRITER

SERVES 4
DIFFICULTY

SCAMPI-BISQUE
17.6 oz (500 g) small scampi
3.5 oz (100 g) white onions, diced
1.8 oz (50 g) carrots, diced
1.8 oz (50 g) celery, diced
1.8 oz (50 g) shallots, diced
1 garlic clove, minced
5.3 oz (150 g) fennel, diced
⅓ cup (80 ml) brandy
10.6 oz (300 g) Datterino tomatoes, halved
1.8 (50g) oz tomato paste
0.18 oz (5 g) basil
0.18 oz (5 g) thyme
salt & pepper
olive oil

FISH STOCK
2.2 lbs (1 kg) sole fillets
5.3 oz (150 g) celery, diced
5.3 oz (150 g) white onions, diced
3.5 oz (100 g) fennel, diced
10 black peppercorns
3 bay leaves
3 sprigs thyme
2 cups (500 ml) white wine
12 ¾ cups (3 l) water

RISOTTO WITH SCAMPI-CARPACCIO
16 large scampi tails, peeled
2 tbsp extra virgin olive oil
8.5 oz (240 g) Carnaroli rice
½ cup (125 ml) white wine
2 cups (500 ml) scampi bisque
2 cups (500 ml) fish stock
0.5 oz (15 g) shallots, finely chopped
1.4 oz (40 g) alpine butter
1.2 oz (35 g) grated Parmigiano Reggiano
grated orange zest
salt & pepper

TO SERVE
extra virgin olive oil
fresh herbs of choice
Maldon salt

1 SCAMPI-BISQUE
Remove the scampi heads and roast them in the oven until golden brown. In a pot, sauté the diced vegetables (except the tomatoes) in olive oil. Add the roasted scampi, deglaze with brandy, then stir in the tomatoes and tomato paste. Cover with water, bring to a simmer, add the herbs, and let cook for at least an hour. Blend the mixture, strain, and reduce until desired consistency is reached. Season with salt and pepper.

2 FISH STOCK
Combine all ingredients in a large pot and slowly bring to a boil. Skim off any foam that forms on the surface. Simmer for an hour, then strain through a fine cloth.

3 RISOTTO WITH SCAMPI-CARPACCIO
To prepare the scampi carpaccio, place plastic wrap on a work surface, drizzle with 1 tsp olive oil, and arrange two scampi tails on top. Cover with another sheet of plastic wrap and gently flatten with a heavy object. Freeze until firm. Toast the rice in a large pot without oil. Add the white wine and allow it to fully evaporate while stirring constantly. Gradually incorporate the scampi bisque and fish stock, one ladle at a time, stirring continuously. Add the finely chopped shallots and cook over medium heat until the rice is al dente. Stir in the remaining scampi tails, remove from heat, and let rest for a few minutes. Finish with the olive oil, butter, Parmesan, and orange zest. Adjust seasoning with salt and pepper, adding a touch more fish stock if needed.

4 TO SERVE
Spoon the risotto onto a plate and top with the frozen scampi carpaccio, allowing it to gently melt into the warm risotto. Garnish with olive oil, Maldon salt, fresh herbs, and a drizzle of reduced bisque.

ASTICE, CREMA ALL'ARANCIA, INSALATA DI PUNTARELLE E GERMOGLI INVERNALI, ERBETTE DI CAMPO

LOBSTER IN ORANGE CREAM, PUNTARELLE SALAD, SPROUTS, AND WILD HERBS

SERVES 4
DIFFICULTY

4 lobster tails à 14 oz (400g)
8 lobster claws
3.5 oz (100 g) butter
0.7 oz (20 g) thyme
freshly squeezed juice of 2 oranges
0.35 oz (20 g) sour cream
7.1 oz (200 g) puntarelle
7.1 oz (200 g) Treviso radicchio
3.5 oz (100 g) Gorizia rose radicchio
1 tsp (5 ml) apple cider vinegar
sprouts of choice
olive oil (for drizzling)

1 Cook the lobster tails for 3 minutes and the claws for 3 ½ minutes in boiling water, then carefully remove Melt the butter in a pan, add the thyme, and briefly sear the lobster tails and claws.

2 Place the lobster claws in a pot with 2.5 cups water and the orange juice, reduce by half Stir in the sour cream.

3 Sauté the puntarelle in a hot pan and distribute on serving plates Place the lobster tails on top and drizzle with some lobster bisque.

4 Remove the meat from the lobster claws and cut into small pieces Mix with radicchio, sprouts, and apple cider vinegar and arrange on separate plates Drizzle with high-quality olive oil before serving.

RISTORANTE QUADRI

TWO BROTHERS – ONE DREAM TEAM

RISTORANTE QUADRI
PIAZZA SAN MARCO 121
+39 041-522 21 05
alajmo.it/relaischateaux.com

OPENING HOURS:

Wednesday to Friday:
7:00 PM – 10:00 PM
Saturday and Sunday:
12:00 PM – 2:30 PM
and 7:00 PM – 10:00 PM
Closed on Mondays

With the arrival of the Alajmo brothers – a dynamic duo behind top-tier gastronomic ventures such as the three-Michelin-starred La Calandre in Padua and the Royal Mansour in Marrakech – the long-standing rivalry between the two legendary cafés on St. Mark's Square took on a whole new dimension. While Caffè Florian continues to enjoy global fame, Quadriturned the page in 2010 and entered a new era. It's worth remembering that Grancaffè Quadri first opened its doors in 1775, welcoming guests as illustrious as Lord Byron and Alexandre Dumas over the years, rivaling the establishment just across the square. Yet, Quadri always embraced a more understated elegance – until now. Raffaele Alajmo, the visionary, and Massimiliano, the passionate culinary artist – known simply as Raf and Max – have breathed new life into the historic two-story building. The true gem of the establishment is the fine-dining Quadri on the first floor, which, unsurprisingly, quickly earned a Michelin star. Max leads the way, creatively reinterpreting the opulent recipes of the Renaissance for a contemporary audience. At the helm of the kitchen are Executive Chefs Silvio Giavedoni and Sergio Preziosa, supported by Sommelier Giacomo Lorato. Guests can choose from à la carte dishes like lobster with mango, peach, and fennel or opt for a three- or eight-course tasting menu. For a more relaxed take on haute cuisine, the ground-floor Quadrino bistro offers lighter fare – think Club Sandwiches and Caesar Salad with an unmistakable Alajmo touch. In 2018, Grancaffè Quadri underwent a stunning transformation. Design icon and close friend of the Alajmo brothers, Philippe Starck, worked his magic on the slightly timeworn café, simultaneously redesigning the Michelin-starred restaurant and the Quadrino. The result: an enchanting, almost otherworldly space. But the brothers never rest. Their latest venture? Culinary tours through the Venetian lagoon aboard the motor yacht Aqva. The onboard chef, like his colleagues at Quadri, sources ingredients from the brothers' own two-hectare vegetable garden on the island of Certosa. Quadri is a proud member of the Relais & Châteaux association.

Left – A glimpse into Ristorante Quadri, redesigned by star architect Philippe Starck.

Below – Executive Chef Sergio Preziosa presents Renaissance recipes with a contemporary twist.

FAVORITE SPOTS OF SERGIO PREZIOSA

For those unfamiliar with Venice, I highly recommend wandering aimlessly through its labyrinthine streets – that's the best way to stumble upon hidden gems like Bepi Antico 54 da Loris (Salizada del Pistor, Cannaregio 4550), or Osteria Giorgione da Masa (Calle Larga dei Proverbi, Cannaregio 4582a). Among the traditional bacari, I have a special fondness for All'Arco (see p. 220), while for after-dinner drinks, my go-to is the Arcultural experience, don't miss the island of San Lazzaro degli Armeni – a hidden Middle Eastern gem in the heart of the lagoon.

ORTO DI SANT'ERASMO

THE VEGETABLE GARDEN OF SANT'ERASMO

SERVES 4
DIFFICULTY

EGGPLANT PURÉE
14 oz (400 g) round purple eggplants, peeled and diced
1 tbsp extra virgin olive oil
¾ tsp (4 g) salt

TOMATO TARTARE
7 oz (200 g) ripe tomatoes
3.5 oz (100 g) cherry tomatoes (preferably Pachino)
⅛ tsp (1 g) granulated sugar
about 1 tbsp extra virgin olive oil
a pinch of dried oregano (optional)
¾ tsp (2 g) salt

TOMATO WATER
1 lb (500 g) Datterino tomatoes, halved

TOMATO JELLY
⅓ cup (100 ml) tomato water
¼ tsp (1 g) agar-agar
a pinch of salt

PISTACHIO PURÉE
8.8 oz (250 g) ground pistachios
¾ cup (200 ml) still mineral water

BASIL-PISTACHIO PESTO
⅔ cup (150 ml) extra virgin olive oil
5.3 oz (150 g) pine nuts
10.5 oz (300 g) basil leaves
10.5 oz (300 g) pistachio purée
¾ tsp (2 g) salt

TOMATO SAUCE
4.2 oz (120 g) Datterino tomatoes
1 ½ tbsp extra virgin olive oil
¾ tsp (2 g) granulated sugar
1 tsp (1 g) salt

DICED EGGPLANT WITH OREGANO
9.5 oz (270 g) round purple eggplants, sliced into ½-inch-thick rounds
1 ½ tbsp extra virgin olive oil
a pinch of dried oregano
¾ tsp (1 g) salt

TO SERVE
4 pistachios, coarsely chopped
8.5 oz (240 g) Datterino tomatoes, sliced and seasoned with olive oil and salt
8 red onion rings, seasoned with olive oil, salt, and balsamic vinegar
4 black Taggiasca olives, pitted and chopped
¼ oz (6 g) basil leaves
¾ oz (20 g) Pane Carasau (Sardinian flatbread), toasted
Extra virgin olive oil for drizzling

1 EGGPLANT PURÉE
Place the diced eggplants in a glass or ceramic baking dish. Cover the dish and microwave on high until soft.
Pat dry with paper towels to remove excess moisture. Purée with olive oil and salt until smooth.

2 TOMATO TARTARE
Blanch the tomatoes briefly in boiling water, then drain. Peel and deseed them. Finely chop the prepared tomatoes and mix with salt and sugar.
Let the mixture drain in a sieve, discarding the excess liquid.
Drizzle the reserved tomato flesh with olive oil and, if desired, add a pinch of oregano.

3 TOMATO WATER
Blend the tomato halves until completely puréed.
Line a sieve with a clean kitchen towel and place it over a bowl. Pour in the tomato purée. Allow it to drain slowly without pressing, so only the clear tomato water collects in the bowl.

4 TOMATO JELLY
Season the tomato water with salt.
Mix half of the tomato water with the agar-agar, bring to a boil, and stir constantly for 2 minutes. Remove from heat, add the remaining tomato water, and stir well. Pour the mixture into a rectangular mold (about 2 x 1.5 inches) to create a ¼-inch-thick layer. Refrigerate for about 2 hours until set.

5 PISTACHIO PURÉE
Gradually blend the pistachios with the mineral water until smooth.
Pour the mixture into a Pacojet container and freeze at -4°F for at least 24 hours.
Once frozen, process in a Pacojet until creamy.

6 BASIL-PISTACHIO PESTO
Quickly blend the olive oil and pine nuts in a high-powered blender, pausing occasionally to prevent overheating.
Add the basil and salt, then continue blending until smooth.
Incorporate the pistachio purée and blend briefly until fully combined.

7 TOMATO SAUCE
Blend the tomatoes and strain through a fine sieve.
Emulsify with olive oil, sugar, and salt.

8 DICED EGGPLANT WITH OREGANO
Steam the eggplant slices for 2 minutes until tender. Cut into ½-inch cubes and season with olive oil, oregano, and salt.

9 TO SERVE
Spoon 1 tbsp of eggplant purée into a bowl.
Top with some basil-pistachio pesto and the chopped pistachios.
Coat the Datterino tomatoes with tomato jelly.
Arrange the tomato tartare, tomato sauce, and jelly-coated Datterino tomatoes alongside.
Garnish with diced eggplant, onion rings, olives, and basil leaves.
Place a piece of warm Pane Carasau on top and drizzle with olive oil before serving.

MEZZI PACCHERI CON CRUDO DI PESCE E SALSA DI DATTERINI

MEZZI PACCHERI WITH RAW FISH, AND DATTERINO TOMATO SAUCE

SERVES 3
DIFFICULTY

MEZZI PACCHERI
11 oz (320 g) Mezzi Paccheri
2 tbsp extra virgin olive oil
1 tsp (5 ml) soy sauce
1 small fresh chili, finely chopped
1 ½ tsp (4 g) basil leaves, finely sliced
Salt

FISH TARTARE
2.8 oz (80 g) raw red prawn tails
2.8 oz (80 g) raw langoustine tails
2.8 oz (80 g) raw amberjack fillet
2.8 oz (80 g) raw red mullet fillet
2.8 oz (80 g) raw lobster meat
3 tbsp (40 g) extra virgin olive oil
a dash of lemon juice
Salt

TOMATO SAUCE
10.5 oz (300 g) Datterino tomatoes
3 ½ tbsp (50 g) extra virgin olive oil
salt

TO SERVE
Tomato jelly (see p. 28)
A pinch of ground black cumin
12 basil leaves
¾ oz (20 g) salted capers, rinsed

1 **COOKING THE MEZZI PACCHERI**
Cook the pasta in plenty of boiling salted water until al dente. Drain, rinse under cold running water, and pat dry with paper towels.
Toss with olive oil, soy sauce, chili, basil, and salt.

2 **PREPARING THE FISH TARTARE**
Cut the raw fish into small cubes and place them in a bowl. Gently mix with olive oil, lemon juice, and salt.

3 **MAKING THE TOMATO SAUCE**
Blend the tomatoes and strain them through a fine sieve. Emulsify the mixture with olive oil and salt.

4 **TO SERVE**
Fill the Paccheri with the raw fish mixture and arrange them in a cold, shallow dish. Garnish with tomato jelly, black cumin, basil, and capers. Spoon the tomato sauce alongside and serve.

Top – Originally from Vieste in Apulia: the charismatic chef Giuseppe Ricci.

Bottom – From the garden terrace, one can see the Isola San Giorgio Maggiore in the distance.

GIO'S RESTAURANT

PHOENIX FROM THE ASHES

**GIO'S RESTAURANT
& TERRACE
AT THE ST. REGIS VENICE
+39 041-240 00 01**
giosrestaurantvenice.com

OPENING HOURS:

Daily 7:00 AM – 10:30 AM
12:30 PM – 2:45 PM
7:00 PM – 10:00 PM

It couldn't have been worse: three months after the glamorous opening of the St. Regis Hotel, just a stone's throw from St. Mark's Square in August 2019, a once-in-a-century flood submerged Venice. The garden and terrace on the banks of the Grand Canal were destroyed – flower pots drifted as far as Teatro La Fenice. Just as everything was hastily rebuilt, the 2020 lockdown followed. Today, sitting in the romantic garden amid rose bushes – with a view of the Chiesa della Salute on the opposite bank of the canal – it is hard to imagine what happened. The lovingly restored terrace is also the outdoor area of Gio's restaurant, a contemporary haven of comfort that is open all day – not only for hotel guests. The philosophy is simple: the finest ingredients, sourced as locally as possible, transformed into modern dishes deeply rooted in Italian and Venetian culinary traditions. The day begins with baking a wide selection of fresh breads, served at breakfast in a garden that once inspired Claude Monet to create masterpieces. Representatives of Venice's vibrant art scene and Biennale visitors love the relaxed ambiance and uncomplicated cuisine of the St. Regis Bar for lunch. Browsing the menu, one might spontaneously crave Spaghetti ai tre pomodori or sea bass from the lagoon with spinach and celery purée. Those with a bigger appetite can opt for a three-course tasting menu, with or without wine pairing. In the evening, Chef Giuseppe Ricci takes center stage. Dishes are served on hand-painted Ginori 1735 porcelain, crafted in Italy for 300 years. The preferred choice is the five-course tasting menu, offering a representative cross-section of Ricci's imaginative culinary world. Originally from the seaside town of Vieste in Apulia, he first entered the hospitality industry at his parents' request, only to quickly discover his passion for cooking. On his journey to Venice, he spent four years at The Dorchester in London, gained experience at Acanto in Milan, and, before taking the helm at Gio's, had an invaluable tenure under Giovanni Ciresa, then executive chef at Bauer Venice. During this time, he realized how much his culinary excellence depended on sourcing the right suppliers. Finding them was hard work, but it clearly paid off. Guests booking his cooking class accompany him to the Rialto Market, his vegetable supplier on the island of Vignole, and a fisherman in Murano. This virtuoso's culinary talent is mirrored in a meticulously curated art collection displayed throughout the hotel. The absolute eye-catcher is the "White Chandelier" by Ai Weiwei in the Grand Salon, a masterpiece born from collaboration with the renowned Studio Berengo in Murano.

BOTTONI DI PASTA POVERA RIPIENI DI BACCALÀ ALLA VICENTINA, ZOTOI E LEVISTICO

BOTTONI WITH VICENZA-STYLE SALTED COD, BABY SQUID, AND LOVAGE

SERVES 4
DIFFICULTY

PASTA DOUGH
2 cups (250 g) semolina flour
2 cups (250 g) fine durum wheat flour
2 tbsp (25 g) softened butter
⅔ cup (150 ml) water at 104°F

FILLING
7 oz (200 g) salted cod (baccalà)
¼ cup (30 g) all-purpose flour
1 tbsp grapeseed oil
4 anchovy fillets
1.8 oz (50 g) white onions, finely diced
2 bay leaves
2 tbsp (30 ml) white wine
1 oz (25 g) grated Parmigiano Reggiano
1 tsp (5 g) chopped parsley
3.5 oz (100 g) heavy cream
1 ⅔ cups (400 ml) milk
4 tbsp olive oil
1 pinch nutmeg
salt & pepper

FISH STOCK
2.2 lbs (1 kg) white fish bones
1.8 oz (50 g) white onions, roughly chopped
0.7 oz (20 g) shallots, roughly chopped
1.8 oz (50 g) celery stalks, chopped
1.8 oz (50 g) fennel, chopped

LOVAGE OIL
1.8 oz (50 g) lovage
2 tbsp (25 ml) grapeseed oil

BABY SQUID (ZOTOI)
5 baby squid
1 tbsp olive oil
1 pinch salt
1 pinch pepper

TO SERVE
0.1 oz (3 g) cubeb pepper
2 tbsp truffle butter
zest of ½ organic lemon
5 lovage leaves

1 **PASTA DOUGH**
Combine all ingredients in a stand mixer and knead for 4 to 6 minutes until a homogeneous dough forms

2 **BACCALÀ**
Soak the salted cod in cold water for 4 hours, then refrigerate overnight at 39°F.
On the day of preparation, remove from the liquid and pat dry. Remove bones, season with salt and pepper, and dust with flour. Heat grapeseed oil in a saucepan, add anchovies, and melt over low heat. Add onions and bay leaves, sauté, then deglaze with white wine. Sprinkle onions, then Parmesan, and finally parsley over the baccalà. Cut into 2.5-inch thick slices, place in a deep baking tray, cover with cream, milk, and olive oil, then cover with parchment and foil.
Bake at 285°F for about 3 hours. Drain cooking liquid, pass the solid mixture through a meat grinder with a coarse blade. If needed, add some cooking liquid for a smooth consistency. Season with nutmeg, salt, and pepper.

3 **BOTTONI**
Roll out the dough to 0.2 inches thick and cut 1.5-inch circles. Place a teaspoon of filling in the center of each round, cover with another round, and seal the edges. Sprinkle a baking sheet with semolina and place the bottoni on it until further use.

4 **FISH STOCK**
Rinse fish bones under cold running water. Bring water to a boil in a tall pot, blanch the bones without breaking them, then drain and shock in ice water. Transfer to a large pot, add vegetables, cover with cold water, and simmer over medium heat for about 1 hour without stirring. Strain through a fine sieve.

5 **LOVAGE OI**
Blanch the lovage in boiling water, drain, and cool in ice water. Pat dry, then blend with grapeseed oil until smooth. Strain through cheesecloth and transfer to a squeeze bottle.

6 **BABY SQUID**
Clean squid, remove heads, innards, and central bone. Rinse thoroughly, pat dry, season with salt and pepper. Quickly blanch before serving. Heat olive oil in a pan and sear squid for about 3 minutes until golden brown. Drain on paper towels. Serve immediately.

7 **TO SERVE**
Toast cubeb pepper in a dry pan, let cool, and grind. Cook bottoni in fish stock for 3 minutes, drain, and toss in truffle butter. Plate 5 bottoni per dish, garnish with lemon zest and cubeb pepper. Arrange seared baby squid on top, drizzle with lovage oil, and serve.

BRANZINO DI LAGUNA AGLIO, OLIO E PEPERONCINO, SPINACI SALTATI E PURÈ DI SEDANO RAPA

LAGOON SEA BASS WITH GARLIC, OLIVE OIL, AND CHILI, SAUTÉED SPINACH, AND CELERY ROOT PURÉE

SERVES 4
DIFFICULTY

SEA BASS REDUCTION
2.2 lbs (1 kg) sea bass bones
¾ cup (200 ml) water
1.8 oz (50 g) white onions, diced
0.7 oz (20 g) shallots, diced
1.8 oz (50 g) celery stalks, diced
1.8 oz (50 g) fennel, diced

CELERY ROOT PURÉE
2 cups (500 ml) milk
¾ cup (200 ml) heavy cream
8.8 oz (250 g) celery root, diced
2 tbsp olive oil
½ tsp (3 g) salt

GARLIC-CHILI SAUCE
5.3 oz (150 g) garlic, peeled
3.5 oz (100 g) shallots, peeled
2.6 oz (75 g) anchovies
¼ cup (50 ml) white wine
5 tbsp extra virgin olive oil
1 chili pepper

SPINACH
1 tbsp olive oil
1 garlic clove, crushed
17.6 oz (500 g) spinach
½ tsp (3 g) salt

SEA BASS
17 oz (480 g) sea bass fillets
1 tbsp olive oil
4 sprigs thyme
1 garlic clove
1 tsp (5 g) salt

1 **SEA BASS REDUCTION**
Rinse the fish bones under cold running water. Place in a vacuum-sealed bag with water and vegetables, sealing at 80%. Cook sous vide at 183°F for 4 hours, then strain the liquid and reduce it in a rotary evaporator at 158°F for 30 minutes.

2 **CELERY ROOT PURÉE**
Heat milk and cream in a large pot, stirring constantly. Cook celery root until very soft. When it begins to break down, purée with an immersion blender, season with salt, and emulsify with olive oil. Strain through a fine sieve.

3 **GARLIC-CHILI SAUCE**
Blanch garlic and shallots three times in boiling water, changing the water each time. Purée with an immersion blender, then add remaining ingredients and emulsify at high speed. Strain through a clean cloth.

4 **SPINACH**
Heat olive oil and garlic in a large pan. Add spinach and sauté until just wilted. Season with salt.

5 **SEA BASS**
Score the skin of the sea bass, cut into 1.4 oz portions, season with salt, and coat with oil. Sear in a hot pan until a crust forms, then reduce heat. Add thyme and garlic, cover, and allow to cook gently while plating.

6 **TO SERVE**
Spoon a small amount of sea bass reduction onto deep plates. Drizzle with garlic-chili sauce, add a dollop of celery root purée, and arrange three sea bass pieces on top. Place the sautéed spinach around the fish, drizzle with additional reduction, and serve.

OSTERIA DA CARLA

FROM THE HEART TO THE STOVE

OSTERIA DA CARLA
CORTE CONTARINA
SAN MARCO 1535
+39 041-523 78 55
osteriadacarla.it

OPENING HOURS:

Monday to Saturday
9:00 AM – 10:30 PM
Sunday closed

When the Siviero family took over this historic Osteria in 1988 – one of the oldest in the city – they inherited a difficult legacy. They struggled to balance the tradition of a long-established tavern with the demands of modern times. It was not until 2016, when Michela Siviero took the helm after 30 years, that the tide turned. With the help of her son Giovanni and an ambitious young team, she breathed new life into the concept of an Osteria, redesigned the historic Venetian building, and masterfully combined tradition with modernity. Today, it is Giacomo and Giannina who welcome guests with both professionalism and a personal touch.

Head chef Fosca Scarpa grew up on the Lido, a narrow island between the lagoon and the sea. She understands the island's unpredictable weather conditions and the changing of the seasons. Even as a young woman, she discovered her passion for the local ingredients of her homeland and began experimenting with vegetable cultivation. In the early 2000s, she found work in a seafood restaurant on the mainland, where she developed her skills as a self-taught chef. And she succeeded. Her cuisine is enriched by the freshest and finest ingredients from the markets in Chioggia and Venice. Her signature dish: Plateau Royal, a selection of the finest fish and seafood from the lagoon, beautifully arranged on a plate. Stints in the Maldives and New York expanded her experience, while her keen artistic sense inspires her to create imaginative and stunning plate presentations. Fosca firmly believes that ideas are born in the mind, settle in the heart, and finally reach the plate. After 15 years in Mestre, she decided to move to Venice and take over the Osteria da Carla. She immediately felt at home in this harmonious family-run business. Here, a robust red wine is paired with a mixed platter of cured meats from local suppliers or a selection of regional cheeses served with mostarda. And perhaps afterward, a "Karbor" risotto with smoked eel, Castelmagno cheese, farmhouse butter, and lime gel. To finish, a few homemade cookies with a glass of sweet dessert wine, such as Passito di Pantelleria or Vendemmia Tardiva Orvieto. Buon Appetito!

Left – Ladies in Black: Host Michela Giugie and Chef Fosca Scarpa.

Below – Red wines release their bouquet in voluminous glasses.

Bottom – A traditional tavern transformed into a stylish restaurant.

RISOTTO CON ANGUILLA AFFUMICATA BOTÌRO DI PRIMIERO, CASTELMAGNOE GEL DI LIME

RISOTTO WITH SMOKED EEL, BOTÌRO DI PRIMIERO (ALPINE BUTTER), CASTELMAGNO, AND LIME GEL

SERVES 2
DIFFICULTY

RISOTTO
1 tbsp olive oil
4.2 oz (120 g) Arborio rice
vegetable broth

SMOKED EEL
1 eel
cherry wood

CASTELMAGNO CREAM
5.3 oz (150 g) grated Castelmagno cheese
10.6 oz (300 g) heavy cream

LIME GEL
juice of 2 limes
2 tbsp (20 g) agar-agar

TO SERVE
Botìro di Primiero butter
(or raw milk butter substitute)

1 **RISOTTO**
Heat the olive oil in a pot. Add the rice and stir for 1–2 minutes until translucent. Deglaze with enough broth to cover the rice. Simmer over low heat, stirring occasionally.
As the liquid is absorbed, gradually add more broth, stirring occasionally. Always add the next portion of broth only after the rice has absorbed the previous one. Cook for a total of 30–35 minutes until the rice is tender.

2 **SMOKED EEL**
Cut the eel into pieces and smoke over cherry wood in a container.

3 **CASTELMAGNO CREAM**
Melt the grated cheese in the heavy cream over a water bath, stirring constantly at a low temperature, until a smooth mixture forms.

4 **LIME GEL**
Mix the lime juice with agar-agar, bring to a boil, and cook while stirring for 2 minutes. Let cool until the mixture gels.

5 **TO SERVE**
Divide the risotto into deep plates and mix with a little Botìro di Primiero butter. Arrange pieces of smoked eel on top, drizzle with Castelmagno cream and lime gel, and serve.

FAVORITE SPOTS OF FOSCA SCARPA

I am a regular at Trattoria dal Vittoria 1938, and I admire Nicolò Trento for his fusion dishes inspired by his travels in Asia (Calle de le Chioverette, Santa Croce 745). And if I have time on the weekend, I take a trip to the island of Pellestrina to enjoy one of the fantastic seafood dishes at Da Celeste.

GONDOLA
179

HOTEL MARCONI
PIZZA

RESTAURANT ANTICO MARTINI

IN POLE POSITION

ANTICO MARTINI
CALLE DEL CAFFETTIER
SAN MARCO 2007
+39 041-522 41 21
anticomartini.com

OPENING HOURS:

Monday to Sunday
11:00 AM – 12:00 AM

Looking back to the year 1720: On the slightly secluded Campo San Fantin, a coffee house opened in the former residence of Admiral Vettor Pisani. A cherished tradition, as coffee – both a luxury and a remedy – had long been one of the Venetian merchants' key commodities alongside exotic spices. Not long after, in May 1792, the Serenissima underlined its role as an international music metropolis with the opening of the Teatro La Fenice. It didn't take long before artists, singers, and composers made the neighboring café their second home. Its success story was interrupted by the devastation of two world wars. When it finally reopened in 1952 under the name Antico Martini as a restaurant looking toward a better future, only the piano remained as a reminder of the days when American soldiers were entertained here. In its new role, Antico Martini quickly became a hotspot for artists, royals, and celebrities, including Arthur Rubinstein, Jean Cocteau, and the Windsors. Its connection to the neighboring opera house certainly played a role, but it was also the outstanding quality of the cuisine that regularly received praise from renowned food critics. When a well-known Venetian entrepreneur took over in 2006, the city's fine dining classic got another boost. The elegant interior was enhanced with additional masterpieces by local artists and handmade lamps from the iconic Venetian brand Fortuny. Guests enjoy their aperitif in the romantic patio, dine in one of the three wood-paneled dining rooms, or on the glass-covered terrace overlooking Teatro La Fenice. The kitchen's philosophy has also been redefined. Hardly a day goes by without the team experimenting with new recipes, reviving Habsburg-era desserts like strudel, chocolate cake, or meringue. Chef Raffaele Dal Pan gained international experience at Harry's Bar in Monte Carlo and with passionate chefs in Japan before taking over the Antico Martini kitchen. His team consists mostly of Venetians, well-versed in preparing local fish and seafood. The heart of the house is Fiore Fabbro, who honed his charm, expertise, and people skills in some of Italy's finest restaurants before becoming host of Antico Martini in 2014.

Left – Gained experience worldwide and returned to Venice: Chef Raffaele dal Pan.

Below – Theatergoers are frequent guests here, before or after a performance at the neighboring Teatro La Fenice.

FAVORITE SPOTS OF FIORE FABBRO

In spring and fall, I enjoy a late morning walk along the Zattere promenade and a light lunch at Restaurant Lineadombra (see p. 168). My favorite place for an aperitif at sunset is the rooftop terrace of the Danieli (Riva degll Schiavoni, Castello 4196). When visiting the lagoon islands, I always stop at Al Gatto Nero on Burano (see p. 198).

FIORI DI ZUCCHINA FARCITI CON RICOTTA AL PESTO DI BASILICO

ZUCCHINI BLOSSOMS STUFFED WITH RICOTTA, AND BASIL PESTO

SERVES 4
DIFFICULTY

STUFFED ZUCCHINI BLOSSOMS
14 oz (400 g) ricotta
4 tbsp pesto Genovese
1 oz (30 g) grated Parmigiano
12 zucchini blossoms
salt & pepper

BARCHETTE
0.9 oz (25 g) phyllo dough

CROSTINI
½ baguette

CREAM
1 zucchini
4 tbsp pumpkin seeds
2 tbsp sesame seeds
1 tbsp cinnamon
1 tbsp coriander
1.8 oz (50 g) roasted potatoes
1 tsp sugar
⅓ cup (80 ml) extra virgin olive oil
salt & pepper

1 **ZUCCHINI BLOSSOMS**
Combine ricotta, pesto, and Parmesan in a bowl and whisk until smooth. Season with salt and pepper, then transfer to a piping bag.
Gently remove the stems and stamens from the blossoms without damaging them. Pipe the filling evenly into each blossom.

2 **BARCHETTE**
Cut the dough into 4 pieces, drape over round aluminum molds, and bake at 340°F for 20 minutes until golden brown.

3 **CROSTINI**
Slice the baguette into 24 thin pieces, place on a baking sheet, and toast until golden brown.

4 **CREAM**
Slice only the green part of the zucchini, blanch for 1 minute, then cool in ice water. Roast pumpkin seeds and sesame seeds in the oven, then set aside 1 tbsp of pumpkin seeds. Blend all remaining ingredients until smooth, seasoning with salt and pepper.

5 **TO SERVE**
Spread half the crostini with the cream and place another crostini on top. Lightly sear the zucchini blossoms in a non-stick pan. Arrange 3 blossoms per plate, garnishing with pumpkin seeds.
Place a barchetta in the center of each plate, fill with 3 crostini, and arrange the zucchini blossoms alongside. Sprinkle with remaining pumpkin seeds and drizzle with olive oil before serving.

FILETTO DI BRANZINO AL LIME, PURÈ DI PATATE E SALICORNIA DORATA

SEA BASS FILLET WITH LIME SAUCE, MASHED POTATOES, AND CRISPY SALICORNIA

SERVES 4
DIFFICULTY

LIME SAUCE
2 tbsp extra virgin olive oil
2.8 oz (80 g) celeriac, chopped
2.8 oz (80 g) potatoes, chopped
2 organic limes
3 tbsp (40 ml) white wine
1 cup (250 ml) fish stock
1.8 oz (50 g) butter
salt & pepper

SALICORNIA
4.2 oz (200 g) salicornia (sea beans)
milk
flour
2 cups (500 ml) peanut oil

MASHED POTATOES
1.1 lbs (500 g) potatoes
2.8 oz (80 g) butter
⅔ cup (150 ml) milk
1 tbsp chopped fennel
salt

SEA BASS FILLET
4 skin-on sea bass fillets (5–7 oz; 150-200g each)
juice of 1 organic lemon
3 tbsp olive oil
salt & freshly ground black pepper

1 **LIME SAUCE**
Heat olive oil in a pot, sauté celeriac and potatoes. Thinly peel limes, avoiding the bitter white pith. Slice the peels finely and set aside.
Blanch limes twice in 3/4 cup water, reserving the water.
Juice the blanched limes and mix with reserved water. Reduce the lime juice mixture and white wine by half.
Add fish stock, sautéed vegetables, lime zest, and butter. Season with salt and pepper, blend until smooth, and strain.

2 **MASHED POTATOES**
Boil potatoes in salted water, drain, and mash. Stir in butter, milk, and fennel, seasoning with salt.

3 **SALICORNIA**
Soak salicornia in milk for 1–2 hours.
Drain, dust with flour, and fry in hot peanut oil until crispy.

4 **SEA BASS FILLET**
Rinse fillets, pat dry, and remove any bones. Drizzle flesh side with lemon juice. Heat olive oil in a pan, sear fillets skin-side down for 3–5 minutes, then flip and cook another 2–3 minutes. Season with salt and pepper.

5 **TO SERVE**
Plate the sea bass fillets with lime sauce, mashed potatoes, and crispy salicornia.
Serve immediately.

VINO VINO

FOR THE LOVE OF WINE

VINO VINO
OSTERIA & WINE BAR
PONTE DELLE VESTE
SAN MARCO 2007/A
+39 041-241 76 88
vinovinowinebar.com

OPENING HOURS:

Daily 11:30 AM – 11:30 PM

The "little brother" shares the same owner and kitchen as the neighboring Antico Martini, though at a more casual level. Compared to its upscale counterpart, this beloved wine bar is smaller, cozier rather than elegant, embracing the philosophy of a simple osteria with good food and an impressive wine selection. The wooden paneling dates back to the 1920s. A significant number of the roughly 200 wine labels are available by the glass.

Around midday, the clientele consists of passersby who prefer a simple pasta dish – perhaps spaghetti carbonara or fusilli al pomodoro – or a pizza such as Margherita or one with ham and mushrooms. Here, pizza is often paired with beer. However, many guests come simply to sample one or two wines. Among the finest whites: Elianto Custoza Superiore, Lugana Classico Santa Cristina, and Sur Sur Grillo from Donna Fugata winery. Among the top reds are Nobile di Montepulciano and Amarone Valpolicella Classico. Wine drinking has a long tradition in Venice. In earlier times, the less affluent would dilute water with a splash of wine bought from mobile wine vendors on St. Mark's Square. This evolved into the tradition of the bacari, along with the habit of enjoying a glass as early as late morning. During the days of the Serenissima Republic, there was a state alcohol monopoly, and wines from Istria and Dalmatia were heavily taxed – affordable only to the wealthy. This changed in the 19th century when wines from Apulia first arrived in Venice. Today, more than 50,000 100-milliliter glasses of wine from across Italy are served daily in the bacari. Beyond the traditional taverns, modern wine bars are emerging, offering guests not only seating but also menus featuring warm dishes alongside small bites – just like Vino Vino. For a light snack, pair a glass of wine from Trentino, Friuli, Veneto, Piave, or the Puster Valley with prosciutto & melon, a cheese platter, or the famous sarde in saor. Many guests combine an evening at Teatro La Fenice with a visit to Vino Vino – grabbing a quick bite before the performance and enjoying a full meal afterward, often opting for the pesce del giorno or fegato alla veneziana. Something sweet to finish – just like at its bigger sibling next door – is an absolute must. Reservations highly recommended!

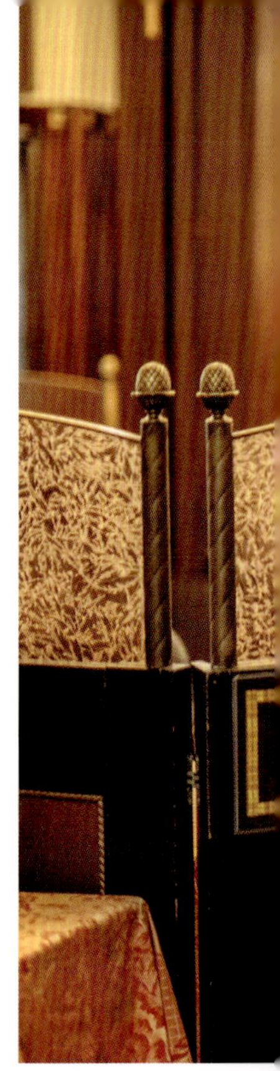

Far left – The osteria offers seating for guests seeking a more intimate setting.

Left – Raffaele Dal Pan is also responsible for the kitchen at the neighboring sister restaurant, Antico Martini.

Below – A variety of Fortuny lamps create ambiance and perfect lighting.

CASTRAURE FRITTE IN CIALDA AI CARCIOFI

FRIED ARTICHOKES IN AN ARTICHOKE WAFER

SERVES 4
DIFFICULTY

ARTICHOKES
8 artichokes
4 cups (1 l) vegetable oil

ARTICHOKE WAFERS
8 peeled artichoke stems
1 tsp quinoa
1 oz (30 g) potato

TO SERVE
salt
10 drops Worcestershire sauce

1 **ARTICHOKES**
Halve the artichokes lengthwise, removing the tough outer leaves and stems.
Set stems aside for the artichoke wafers.
Heat the oil in a deep pan and fry the artichokes until golden brown.

2 **ARTICHOKE WAFERS**
Place all ingredients in a pot, add about 3/4 cup water, and bring to a boil. Puree the mixture and spread thinly onto a silicone mat. Let dry in the oven at low temperature, then drape over 4 cups or muffin tins and continue drying. Finally, fry for a few seconds.

3 **TO SERVE**
Arrange the fried artichokes in the wafers, season with salt and Worcestershire sauce, and serve immediately.

CRACKERS DI PASTA FILLO CON CARPACCIO DI MANZO

PHYLLO CRACKERS WITH BEEF CARPACCIO

SERVES 1
DIFFICULTY

BEEF CARPACCIO
2.8 oz (80 g) beef tenderloin

CARPACCIO SAUCE
2 heaping tbsp mayonnaise
1 heaping tbsp mustard
10 drops Worcestershire sauce

PHYLLO CRACKERS
1 sheet phyllo dough (12 x 12 inches)
about 0.7 oz (20 g) melted butter
1 heaping tbsp grated Parmigiano Reggiano

1 **BEEF CARPACCIO**
Cut the beef tenderloin into 8 thin slices.
Place each slice between two sheets of parchment paper and pound as thin as possible with a meat mallet.

2 **CARPACCIO SAUCE**
Whisk all ingredients together in a bowl until smooth.

3 **PHYLLO CRACKERS**
Lay out the phyllo dough and brush with melted butter. Sprinkle with Parmesan and cut into 8 equal pieces.
Place on a greased baking sheet and bake at 340°F for 3 minutes until crispy.
Let cool.

4 **TO SERVE**
Place the meat slices on the crackers and drizzle the sauce in thin streaks over them.

CANNOLI DI POLENTA FARCITI CON BACCALÀ MANTECATO

POLENTA CANNELONI FILLED WITH SALTCOD AND CARPACCIO

SERVES 4
DIFFICULTY

BACCALÀ MANTECATO
5 ⅓ oz (150 g) salt cod
1 ¼ cups (300 ml) milk
⅓ cup (80 ml) sunflower oil
1 crushed anchovy
salt & pepper

POLENTA CANNOLI
5 ⅓ oz (150 g) cold polenta

1 **BACCALÀ MANTECATO**
Remove the skin, bones, and vertebrae from the salt cod. Place the salt cod in a pot with milk, adding a little water if necessary, and simmer for 40 minutes. Drain, reserving some of the cooking liquid. Transfer the salt cod to a concave bowl and whisk vigorously while gradually drizzling in the oil. If the mixture becomes too thick, incorporate small amounts of the reserved cooking liquid. Add the anchovy and season with salt and pepper.

2 **POLENTA CANNOLI**
Place the polenta in a tall mixing cup and blend with an immersion blender, gradually adding water until it reaches the consistency of crêpe batter. Heat a nonstick pan, pour in a thin layer of the mixture, and allow it to set. Wrap around a metal cannoli mold and place on a baking sheet. Repeat with the remaining batter to form 7 more cannoli, then bake in the oven at 265°F for about 10 minutes until crisp.

3 **TO SERVE**
Fill the cooled cannoli with the salt cod cream and serve immediately.

BISTROT DE VENISE

DISHES WITH HISTORY

BISTROT DE VENISE
CALLE DEI FABBRI
SAN MARCO 4685
+39 041-523 66 51
bistrotdevenise.com

OPENING HOURS:

Daily 12:00 PM – 3:00 PM
and 7:00 PM – 11:30 PM
Bar open daily 11:00 AM – 11:00 PM

Before Carlo, Sergio, and Paolo fulfilled their shared dream in 1993, they delved deep into the history of the city, always in relation to its culinary traditions. They unearthed long-forgotten recipes, rediscovered rare wines, and collected stories. "A life without curiosity is not worth living," is also the motto of chef Stefano Novello, and his career path confirms it. As a young man, he had the opportunity to work alongside culinary legends such as Giorgio Locatelli, Marcus Wareing, and Gordon Ramsay in London. This was followed by an adventurous exploration of the culture and cuisine of Australia before he eventually arrived in Venice. His vast knowledge of food history and development led him to work as a consultant for various restaurants, helping chefs craft their menus and develop new recipes. Since 2021, he has taken the helm of the kitchen at Bistrot de Venise, where every dish tells a story. The marinated sturgeon, for example, has its origins in the Opera dell'Arte del Cucinare, written by composer Bartolomeo Scappi in the 16th century, while the recipe for Linguine alla Buzzara comes from Dalmatian-Venetian cuisine. Some dishes were even documented by author and gastronomist Bartolomeo Sacchi in the 15th century. Novello draws inspiration from the era when the mighty Serenissima's ships returned home laden with exotic spices such as coffee, cinnamon, ginger, and lavender.

To get acquainted with the cuisine, the three-course lunch menu is an excellent choice. Highlights from the menu include veal tongue with Venetian mustard fruits and green sauce – a recipe from the Cucina del Goldoni (18th century) – or pumpkin carpaccio with candied orange peel and cumin, based on a 14th-century recipe. Guests are welcomed into this extraordinary culinary journey with Vivaldi's music playing softly in the background. Alongside Novello, sommelier Stefano Cipolato takes guests deep into the history of wine, exploring the nuances of terroir and the personality of each winemaker. He was named Sommelier of the Year in Veneto in 2008. The wine cellar at Bistrot de Venise boasts an impressive selection of classic and modern wines. A special tip for couples: Book a night in the Honeymoon Suite or the Mirror Room at Residenzia Bistrot de Venise for a romantic stay.

Far left – An atmospheric fine-dining experience with classical music at Bistrot de Venise.

Left – The two cheerful hosts Paolo Fragiacomo (left) and Giancarlo Modonese.

Below – A striking eyecatcher: the tavern sign in Calle dei Fabri.

FAVORITE SPOTS OF STEFANO NOVELLO

In Venice, as in all of Italy, aperitivo is a cherished moment of the day – a time to relax, enjoy, and connect with family and friends. I love the stylish ambiance of Venetian grand hotels, which are so beautifully intertwined with the city's history. I appreciate the quality of their cocktails and the subtle, attentive service. My favorite locations include the terrace of Hotel Danieli and the Londra Palace Bar at the namesake hotel, both on Riva degli Schiavoni.

RISOTTO COTTO & CRUDO

WITH A BISQUE OF RED SHRIMP

SERVES 4
DIFFICULTY

BLUE CRAB GEL WITH CLEAR VERMOUTH
14 oz (400 g) blue crab meat
¾ cup (200 ml) clear vermouth
agar-agar
salt & white pepper

RISOTTO WITH BISQUE OF RED SHRIMP
2 tbsp extra virgin olive oil
1 carrot, diced
1 onion, chopped
1 celery stalk, chopped
2 garlic cloves, crushed
18 oz (500 g) shrimp shells and heads
½ cup (100 ml) brandy or cognac
2 cups (500 ml) dry white wine
1 bouquet garni (thyme, bay leaves, parsley)
1 ⅓ cups (320 g) Carnaroli rice Riserva S. Massimo
salt & black pepper

PARSLEY OIL
3.5 oz (100 g) parsley leaves
1 cup (250 ml) grapeseed oil
1 pinch salt (optional)

TO SERVE
7 oz (200 g) blue crab gel with clear vermouth
1 ⅓ cups (320 g) Carnaroli rice Riserva S. Massimo, cooked with a bisque of red shrimp

GARNISH
licorice powder
star anise powder
beet powder
4 seared scallops with cocoa butter
4 seared scampi in cocoa butter
4 raw Mazara red shrimp
1 tbsp extra virgin olive oil
maldon salt
parsley oil
borage sprouts
fennel sprouts
1 oz (30 g) katsuobushi
dill essence

1 BLUE CRAB GEL WITH CLEAR VERMOUTH

Season the crab meat lightly with salt and pepper. Gently mix in the vermouth and let marinate in the refrigerator for about 30 minutes.
Distribute the crab meat and liquid evenly in a sous-vide bag and seal airtight. Heat a water bath to 190°F and sous-vide cook for 3 hours.
Strain the liquid and reserve it. Measure the liquid and add agar-agar at a ratio of 1% of the total liquid volume.
Bring the mixture to a boil and simmer for 2–3 minutes. Pour into a flat container, cool to room temperature, then refrigerate until set. Once cooled, blend into a smooth, stable gel.

2 RISOTTO WITH BISQUE OF RED SHRIMP

Heat olive oil in a large pot. Add carrot, onion, celery, and garlic, sautéing until softened and lightly golden. Add the shrimp shells and heads, stirring until lightly browned. Deglaze with brandy or cognac and let it evaporate completely. Add white wine and reduce by half. Add 6 cups cold water and the bouquet garni, bring to a boil, then reduce heat. Let simmer for 30–40 minutes, occasionally skimming foam from the surface. Strain through a fine sieve, pressing out as much liquid as possible. Return strained stock to heat and reduce to desired consistency. Season with salt and pepper.
For risotto, heat oil in a pot. Sauté rice for 1–2 minutes until translucent. Add enough bisque to cover rice. Cook over low heat, stirring frequently. Gradually add more bisque as it is absorbed. Cook for 30–35 minutes until rice is tender.

3 PARSLEY OIL

Blend parsley and oil in a Thermomix at 160°F for 9 minutes. Strain through a fine sieve and store in a dark glass bottle.

4 TO SERVE

Arrange the crab gel around the plate, with the risotto in the center, topped with shrimp bisque cream. Garnish with powders, seared scallops, scampi, and raw shrimp. Drizzle with olive oil, Maldon salt, parsley oil, and sprouts. Finish with a touch of dill essence

TIPS: POWDER

Powders made from solid ingredients are a modern technique for concentrating flavors in an unusual and visually appealing form. They are excellent for adding an intense flavor boost to dishes without introducing moisture. Below is a general guide for making powders from solid ingredients such as vegetables, mushrooms, and herbs, as well as liquids like fruit juices or broths.

1. Selecting the ingredient:
Choose an ingredient with a pronounced flavor that you want to transform into a powder, such as mushrooms, tomatoes, or herbs.
2. Preparation:
Clean and cut the ingredient into small pieces to facilitate drying.
3. Dry:
Oven Spread the pieces on a parchment-lined baking sheet and dry them in the oven at a low temperature of 120 to 140°F for several hours until completely dry. Dehydrator If you have a food dehydrator, follow the manufacturer's instructions to dry the selected ingredient.
4. Grinding:
Once the ingredient is completely dry, use a clean coffee grinder, mortar, or blender to grind it into a fine powder.
5. Sifting:
Sift the powder to remove any coarse particles.
6. Storage:
Store the powder in an airtight container in a cool, dry place to preserve its concentrated aroma.

SAN MARCO

1 ISOLA SAN GIORGIO MAGGIORE

Just one vaporetto stop from St. Mark's Square, this tiny island remains a hidden gem despite belonging to the San Marco district. Measuring just 490 meters long and 320 meters wide, its Benedictine monastery and chapel have preserved a sense of heavenly peace. In its present form, the monastery church was designed by Andrea Palladio. After admiring Tintoretto's "Last Supper," painted just before his death, visitors can ascend to the bell tower – either by stairs or elevator.
At 60 meters high, this campanile offers breathtaking views of the Doge's Palace, the neighboring island of Giudecca, and the vast Venetian Lagoon. The entire complex is managed by the Fondazione Giorgio Cini. Advance booking is required for guided tours of the monastery, church, library, refectory, and a labyrinth of over 3,000 boxwood plants. For a relaxing lunch, the San Giorgio Café offers panini and fresh salads on a scenic terrace. Tel. +39 041 271 02 29, closed Wednesdays, ***cini.it***

2 TERRAZZA APEROL

The Aperol Spritz has never been more popular than today. The bright red liqueur remains a secret formula, but the cocktail itself is easy to make:
Three parts Prosecco, two parts Aperol, a splash of soda water, ice cubes, and an orange slice. For true enthusiasts, the Terrazza Aperol is the go-to spot in Venice. Loved by locals as an after-work hotspot, it also offers a weekend brunch special: Aperol Spritz with three cicchetti, brioche, salad, and a dessert for €25. Campo Santo Stefano, San Marco 2776, Tel. +39 041 301 83,open daily 11:00 AM – Midnight (Winter: until 11:00 PM), ***terrazza-aperol.com***

3 MUSICA AL PALAZZO

Venice has long been a city beloved by musicians and composers. Some, like Antonio Vivaldi, were born here, while others, like Richard Wagner, frequently visited for inspiration.
The Musica a Palazzo concept offers a unique opera experience in the elegant salons of the Barbarigo Minotto Renaissance Palace. Instead of a traditional stage, the performances move through different rooms, creating an immersive setting for Italian opera classics such as "The Barber of Seville" by Gioachino Rossini, "Rigoletto" by Giuseppe Verdi, and "La Traviata" by Verdi. Fondamenta Duodo o Barbarigo, San Marco 2504, Tel. +39 340 971 72 72, ***musica-palazzo.com***

4 THE MERCHANT OF VENICE

A haven for fragrance lovers, this elegant boutique is dedicated to Venetian signature perfumes, including "Maria Callas," created for the 100th birthday of the famous opera diva, and "La Fenice Pour Femme." Recently, the collection has expanded to include body lotions and other beauty products that complement the perfumes. Campo San Fantin, San Marco 1895, Tel. +39 041 296 05 59, open 10:30 AM – 7:30 PM, closed Mondays, ***themerchantof-venice.com***

5 ROSTICCERIA GISLON

Since opening in 1938, Gislon has been a staple among the small bars and delicatessens that offer quick and delicious bites for people on the go. Located between St. Mark's Square and the Rialto, its prime location is just one of its many advantages. The long display case is filled with an unbeatable selection of toasts, tramezzini, and other small snacks.
Locals from the neighborhood stop by for a quick bite at lunchtime, either standing at the counter or sitting upstairs for a simple yet satisfying meal. Visitors swear by the Mozzarella in Carrozza, deep-fried mozzarella sandwiches with options like ham, anchovies, or peperoncino, best enjoyed with an ombra (a small glass of wine) for just €5. Calle de la Bissa, San Marco 5424, Tel. +39 041 522 35 69, open daily 9:00 AM – 9:30 PM. A little closer to St. Mark's Square, the Snack Bar Mio is a tiny yet charming spot with a great selection of small bites and friendly service.Frezzeria, San Marco 1176, Tel. +39 041 523 56 12.

6 HOTEL TIP: BEL SITO

Just a few steps away from the bustling tourist trails, this charming hotel offers peace and tranquility. Its 24 rooms, furnished in traditional Venetian style, feature rare antiques from the 18th century. The small courtyard garden is perfect for recharging. Campo Maria del Giglio, San Marco 2517, Tel. +39 041 522 33 65, rooms from €175 ***hotelbelsitovenezia.***

CAFFÈ-SOCIETY 7

The world's great coffeehouse legends can be counted on two hands. Visiting them is like traveling back in time to an era of cultivated leisure. Whether it's the Tortoni in Buenos Aires, Café New York in Budapest, or Café Central in Vienna, they remain unchanged, unwavering, and indestructible. Everything feels like the past – wood-paneled walls, sparkling chandeliers, ornate stucco ceilings, and uniformed waiters serving pastries and canapés. Venice, too, has upheld its coffeehouse tradition since the 18th century, when it welcomed affluent world travelers with no fewer than 24 cafés on St. Mark's Square. Today, three iconic establishments remain, with Caffè Florian, founded in 1720, standing as the quintessence of Venetian coffeehouse culture. With velvet-upholstered furniture beneath antique mirrors, exquisite chandeliers in themed salons, and classical music from the house orchestra, the steeply priced cappuccino is worth every penny. A memorable souvenir: a monogrammed coffee service. Piazza San Marco 57, Tel. +39 041 520 56 41, ***caffeflorian.com***. For those looking to enjoy their first coffee of the day in the morning sun, the Gran Caffè Quadri, located across the square, is the ideal choice. Established by Giorgio Quadri in the late 18th century, it still exudes the romance of Viennese coffeehouses. Since 2010, it has been part of the Alajmo brothers' culinary empire, blending a casual bistro with fine dining under one roof, and in 2018, it received a thoughtful redesign by star designer Philippe Starck. Piazza San Marco 121, Tel. +39 41 522 21 05, ***alajmo.it***. Caffè Lavena was a favorite haunt of Richard Wagner, who often chatted with Carlo Lavena, a Turin native who had sold chocolates and pastries for years before opening his café in 1860. Today, it remains a popular breakfast spot for those reading their morning newspaper in historic surroundings or enjoying an aperitivo with live orchestra music outside. A standout feature: the enormous Murano glass chandelier by Barovier & Toso. If you just want a quick look, a cappuccino at the bar costs €11.50. Piazza San Marco 133–134, Tel. +39 041 522 40 70, ***caffelavena.it***

CAS TELLO

SERVIZIO
GONDOLE

On special occasions, one can spot historic boats decorated with traditional motifs.

Wherever space allows, wine bars place tables and chairs on the streets.

CASTELLO

On sunny days, people crowd along the Riva degli Schiavoni promenade.

At the border with San Marco, the area is still heavily frequented by tourists, but as you move further east, the character of a traditional working-class neighborhood becomes more evident – though some of the simple, low houses are now used as second homes by mainland Italians and newcomers from around the world. The shipyard of the Arsenale, now only open to the public during the Biennale, has long ceased to be the neighborhood's largest employer. It is hard to imagine the speed at which the Serenissima launched warships in its golden age – with up to 16,000 workers employed here at one time.
Wandering through the small alleys away from the bustling Riva degli Schiavoni, the former anchorage for merchant ships and now home to luxury hotels like the Danieli and Londra Palace, is the best way to experience the area. The island of San Giorgio Maggiore and the Chiesa Maria della Salute across the water are always within sight. Sooner or later, one arrives at picturesque squares

During nighttime gondola rides, illuminated windows provide glimpses into Venetian homes.

A few steps away from the tourist flow, one discovers hidden, idyllic corners.

The oldest pharmacy, "Spezieria All'Ercole D'Oro," belongs to the Sestiere Cannaregio.

such as Campo San Zaccharia, Campo Santa Maria Formosa, or Campo Giovanni e Paolo, where the grand basilica of the same name stands. Under its dome, a funeral service was once held for Igor Stravinsky before he was laid to rest on the island of San Michele. There is significantly more activity along the central Via Giuseppe Garibaldi, where supermarkets, bars, butchers, and bakeries showcase everyday Venetian life. The timeless kiosk Il Gazzettino offers everything from pocket novels to badminton sets.

Local wines mostly originate from the Veneto region.

In a passageway known as Sottoportego, cozy taverns are often tucked away.

RESTAURANT WILDNER

A HOUSE WITH HISTORY

RESTAURANT WILDNER
RIVA DEGLI SCHIAVONI
CASTELLO 4161
+39 041-522 74 63
hotelwildner.com

OPENING HOURS:

Daily from 12:00 PM to 10:00 PM
Closed on Tuesdays

Long before the Fullin family opened a guesthouse in this beautiful old building on the Riva degli Schiavoni, English writer Henry James rented a room on the fourth floor to finish his famous novel The Portrait of a Lady in peace. He raved about the gondolas drifting past on the Grand Canal, the enchanting view of Isola San Giorgio, and the distant lagoon islands that appeared and disappeared depending on the weather. The same charm attracts couples and honeymooners today, who have booked a room at the Pensione Wildner since the 1960s. At first, Nonna Lidia took care of the guests' well-being, and today, in its third generation, Luca Fullin and his sister Benedetta continue the tradition.

Luca focused on the kitchen from the very beginning, while also establishing a trade in natural and organic wines across Italy. Together with his sister, he opened the Restaurant Local. As the head chef of the Restaurant Wildner, he places great emphasis on fresh ingredients. Fish and seafood arrive daily from the Rialto market, as do vegetables and herbs from Sant'Erasmo. Like many of his colleagues, Luca Fullin is committed to preserving traditional Venetian cuisine. A significant historical milestone was the 1431 shipwreck of merchant Piero Querini, which left him stranded on a small island in the North Atlantic. Fishermen from the Lofoten Islands rescued and sheltered him for a time, during which he learned the art of preserving fish. Cod was dried using sun and wind, free of moisture and fat, then broken into pieces and sprinkled with spices before being consumed. The rise of bacalà or stockfish in Venice did not begin until nearly 100 years later, when the Council of Trent declared that believers should abstain from meat on certain days of the week. Bacalà quickly became an ideal travel provision. Today, Bacalà Mantecato – a creamy mousse whipped with olive oil – is found in Venetian bacari and on the menus of traditional restaurants. It is served as a spread on bread or paired with polenta. To ensure this tradition continues, the Dogale Confraternita del Bacalà Mantecato brotherhood was established in 2002.

Left – Luca represents the third generation of the Fullin family as head chef.

Below – Every morning – except Tuesdays – Luca Fullin sources fresh ingredients from the Rialto market for his kitchen.

FAVORITE SPOTS OF LUCA FULLIN

When I have time, I take a vaporetto to the Lido and continue by bus or bike to the fishing village of Malamocco. It is almost untouched, and one can easily imagine what life in the lagoon was like before tourism took over. Aside from the summer beach season, the Lido remains a normal, pleasant place. I also frequently take trips to the island of Vignole and visit the most beautiful vegetable gardens of the lagoon.

BACCALÀ MANTECATO

STOCKFISH MOUSSE AS A SPREAD

SERVES 4
DIFFICULTY

10.5 oz (300g) salted cod with skin
12 ¾ cups (3 l) milk
2 bay leaves
3 anchovy fillets
1 garlic clove
2 cups (500 ml) sunflower oil
salt & pepper

Rinse the salted cod under running water, remove any remaining bones, and soak it in half the milk for 40 minutes. Check again for bones. Cut the fish into pieces, place it in a pot with the remaining milk and bay leaves, ensuring it is fully submerged.
Poach over low heat for about 25 minutes, then drain and let it rest in a sieve.
Shred the fish and place it in a planetary mixer along with the anchovies and garlic. Blend while gradually drizzling in the sunflower oil.
Once the desired consistency is reached, season with salt and pepper and serve.

RISOTTO DI GÒ

FISH RISOTTO FROM BURANO

SERVES 4
DIFFICULTY

7 tbsp olive oil
3 poached garlic cloves
1 onion, chopped
1 celery stalk, chopped
2.2 lbs (1 kg) goby fish, gutted
1 shallot, chopped
8.5 oz (240 g) risotto rice
½ cup (125 ml) white wine
1 tbsp butter
1 tbsp grated Parmigiano Reggiano
1 dash lemon juice
1 bunch parsley, chopped
salt & pepper

Heat 2 tbsp olive oil in a pot and sauté the garlic, onion, and celery. Remove the browned garlic, then add the goby fish. Cover with water and let simmer for about an hour.
Blend everything and strain through a sieve. Return the strained broth to the stove and keep warm.
In a new pot, heat 2 tbsp olive oil and sauté the chopped shallot. Add the rice and toast for a few minutes, then deglaze with white wine. Gradually add the hot broth while stirring constantly, cooking the risotto until creamy.
Finish with the remaining olive oil, butter, Parmesan, lemon juice, salt, and pepper. Garnish with chopped parsley and serve.

RISTORANTE LOCAL

A TRUE LOVE STORY

LOCAL
SALIZZADA DEI GRECI
CASTELLO 3303
+39 041-241 11 28
ristorantelocal.com

OPENING HOURS:

Monday, Friday, and Saturday
12:00 PM – 2:00 PM
and 7:00 PM – 10:00 PM
Thursday and Sunday
7:00 PM – 10:00 PM
Closed on Tuesday and Wednesday

Siblings Luca and Benedetta Fullin, heirs to the Pensione Wildner on the Riva degli Schiavoni, opened the gourmet restaurant Local in 2015. Following in the footsteps of her family's legacy, Benedetta first studied journalism and tourism in Milan before spending seven years in London, gaining experience in marketing and Michelin-starred kitchens. In London, she met Manuel Trevisan, a fellow Venetian. Having trained at Osteria da Cera, Manuel developed a passion for wine. After completing his sommelier certification in London, he followed Benedetta to Venice in 2019, taking over as maître d' and sommelier at Local. By 2024, their partnership extended beyond the business, as the couple celebrated their wedding. Since early 2022, Neapolitan chef Salvatore Sedano has helmed the kitchen. Through a glass wall, guests can watch him at work. His culinary philosophy is built on slow cooking, respecting the delicate nature of fresh vegetables and herbs. His passion for food began at home, leading him to Rome, Los Angeles, and eventually London, where he worked alongside his brother Francesco in the kitchen of Enoteca Turi. From there, he returned to Italy, refining his craft along the Amalfi Coast before finally arriving in Venice, a city he had never visited before. Upon meeting Manuel and Benedetta, he immediately recognized two kindred spirits. Just as they cherish Venice, he holds his hometown of Naples close to his heart. With their guidance, he studied the origins of forgotten recipes and personally visited suppliers across the islands to deepen his understanding of local produce. Today, he masterfully bridges tradition and innovation, offering a fresh perspective on Venetian cuisine. For an introduction to his culinary vision, guests can opt for the four-course lunch menu, with or without wine pairing. Wine selections for the tasting menus are curated by Manuel Trevisan, often influenced by his wife's preferences. He carefully selects five wines for a seven-course menu and a maximum of seven for a nine-course experience. The Local wine cellar showcases an exquisite selection from Italy's premier wine regions, spanning from Alto Adige in the north to Sicily in the far south. The restaurant's interior mirrors this blend of tradition and modernity. The flooring, crafted by Murano glassmakers using countless colored stones, pays homage to Venetian heritage, while minimalist lamps and sleek tables reflect contemporary design. Each table is set with only the essentials – cutlery, glasses, and a water carafe – emphasizing pure quality. When Benedetta and Manuel first introduced their modern, innovative approach to Venetian cuisine, some longtime patrons were skeptical. However, their vision was validated within a year when Local was awarded a Michelin star.

Left – Hosts and kindred spirits: Benedetta Fullin and Manuel Trevisan.

Below – Local products are preserved in jars for the winter.

Bottom – Sleek & stylish: the refined interior of Michelin-starred Local.

GRANCHIO BLU, TACCOLE E COMPOSTA DI LIMONE

BLUE CRAB, SUGAR SNAP PEAS, AND CANDIED LEMON PEEL

SERVES 4
DIFFICULTY

BLUE CRAB
8.8 lbs (4 kg) blue crabs
juice and zest of 2 organic limes
extra virgin olive oil
1.1 lbs (500 g) mussels
3.5 oz (100 g) onions, chopped
3.5 oz (100 g) fennel, chopped
4 kaffir lime leaves
1 stalk lemongrass
1 tsp cardamom seeds
2 cloves
1 tsp fennel seeds
salt

SUGAR SNAP PEAS
1.8 oz (50 g) tapioca pearls
1.1 lbs (500 g) sugar snap peas
1 tbsp extra virgin olive oil
salt

CANDIED LEMON
2 lemons
sugar

TO SERVE
dill
nasturtium flowers

1 **BLUE CRAB**
Blanch half of the crabs in boiling water for a few minutes, then remove the meat. Season with lime juice, lime zest, olive oil, and salt, then set aside.
Heat oil in a large pan and sear the remaining crabs along with the mussels. Add the vegetables and sauté for a few minutes. Add kaffir lime leaves, lemongrass, cardamom, cloves, and fennel seeds. Cover with water and simmer for about 2 hours. Strain the bisque through a fine cloth and bring to a brief boil again.

2 **SUGAR SNAP PEAS**
Select the smallest, most tender sugar snap peas and blanch them briefly in lightly salted water. Immediately cool in ice water and pat dry with a clean towel.
Using a kitchen torch, lightly char both sides and cut into small diamonds.
Drain the larger snap peas using a sieve. Meanwhile, cook the tapioca pearls in water, drain, and let them soak in the blue crab bisque, seasoned with a bit of salt and extra virgin olive oil.

3 **CANDIED LEMON**
Thinly peel the lemons. Blanch the peels briefly in boiling water, drain, and pat dry with paper towels. Sprinkle with sugar and dry in a dehydrator at 160°F for about 2 hours. When vacuum-sealed, the candied lemon peel will keep for at least a week in the refrigerator.

4 **TO SERVE**
Fill a deep plate with the tapioca pearl and blue crab bisque. Place the crab meat on top. Arrange the sugar snap peas and finely chopped candied lemon on the side. Garnish with dill and nasturtium flowers, then serve.

FAVORITE SPOTS OF BENEDETTA FULLIN AND MANUEL TREVISAN

For us Venetians, the lagoon islands are the best place to escape daily stress. On Sundays, for example, we love visiting Malamocco. This small fishing village on the southern tip of Lido is always worth a stroll before we enjoy lunch at Al Ponte di Borgo da Mauretto. It's a rustic seafood tavern, beloved by locals and widely known for its exceptional shellfish (Calle Merceria 27, Malamocco).

TRATTORIA CORTE SCONTA

FROM LOCAL TAVERN TO CULINARY INSTITUTION

TRATTORIA CORTE SCONTA
CALLE DEL PESTRIN
CASTELLO 3886
+39 041-522 70 24
cortescontave.com

OPENING HOURS:

Tuesday to Saturday
12:30 PM – 2:00 PM
and 7:00 PM – 9:30 PM
Closed Sunday and Monday

L

Like so many great stories, this one began with two friends sharing a dream. In this case, renowned Venetian architect and urban planner Claudio Proietto and his friend Giampiero Tegon, a hotel concierge with a passion for hospitality. Their wives, Rita and Lena, supported the idea, and so an experiment in gastronomy began. At first, Corte Sconta was just a simple neighborhood tavern, serving a few local wines. Regulars would sometimes bring their own food, ordering just a glass to accompany their meal at one of the rustic wooden tables – especially in the colder months, when many homes were still without heating. In summer, the leafy, grapevine-covered courtyard became a cherished retreat. Over time, traditions evolved. Neighbors still stopped by to play cards with Claudio, but more often, they came for the excellent home-style cuisine. Before long, Corte Sconta had earned its place among Venice's best bacari and wine bars, drawing in notable guests like Mel Brooks, Mick Jagger, Lou Reed, and Italian heartthrob Marcello Mastroianni. Word of the small eatery, well-hidden in a quiet corner of the Castello district and far from the usual tourist routes, spread fast. Reservations soon became essential – a rule that still holds today. Through the years, Corte Sconta has remained a family-run business, now led by Marco Proietto since 2019, alongside members of both founding families and head chef Julio Infante Perez. Guests can now choose from a selection of antipasti, primi, and secondi, with the antipasti following the refined tradition of Venetian cicchetti. Their take on sarde in saor sees the sardines delicately salted and the onions gently steamed before being marinated with raisins and pine nuts in mild vinegar. Even baccalà mantecato, typically a rustic stockfish purée, is transformed into a light and elegant delicacy here. The extensive wine list features top Italian labels alongside carefully selected European wines, including German Riesling, Austrian Grüner Veltliner, Swiss Fendant, Greek Assyrtiko, and French Sancerre. The trattoria's exterior remains unchanged from the design created years ago by acclaimed local architect Sergio Ballini – unpretentious and understated, with pale walls beneath dark wooden beams.

Far left – The trattoria's charm is preserved
without white tablecloths.

Left – Marco Proietto still gets occasional help from his mother, Rita.

Below – Even Mick Jagger found his way to the hidden Calle del Pestrin.

SAUTÉ DI VONGOLE E COZZE

SAUTÉED CLAMS AND MUSSELS

SERVES 2
DIFFICULTY

2 tbsp olive oil
0.7 oz (20 g) ginger
½ tbsp minced garlic
4.4 lbs (2 kg) clams and mussels, cleaned
white pepper
1 ¼ cups (300 ml) white wine

TO SERVE
chopped parsley
lemon wedges

1 Heat the oil in a pan. Add the garlic and ginger, sauté for a few seconds. Add the clams and mussels, sear lightly, and season with white pepper. Deglaze with white wine and add 13.5 fl oz of water. Cover the pan and cook over high heat for 3–5 minutes. Discard any unopened shells.

2 **TO SERVE**
Divide the shellfish onto plates, sprinkle with parsley, and garnish with lemon wedges before serving.

ZABAIONE

TRADITIONAL ITALIAN MARSALA CUSTARD

SERVES 6
DIFFICULTY

¼ cup (50 g) sugar
½ cup (100 g) egg yolks
¼ cup (50 g) sugar
½ cup (100 g) whole eggs
1 tbsp (15 g) cornstarch
¾ cup (200 ml) Marsala
Zest of ⅓ organic lemon
½ cup (100 g) egg whites
½ cup (100 g) sugar
salt

1 Bring ¼ cup sugar and 1 ½ tbsp water to a boil. Whisk the egg yolks with the sugar mixture until light and fluffy. Bring another ¼ cup sugar and 1 ½ tbsp water to a boil. Beat the whole eggs with the sugar mixture, cornstarch, and a pinch of salt until frothy. Combine with the egg yolk mixture, add the Marsala and lemon zest, and blend until smooth.

2 Heat the mixture in a water bath at 175°F (80°C), stirring constantly. Beat the egg whites with ½ cup sugar until stiff peaks form, then gently fold into the mixture.

3 **TO SERVE**
Serve the Zabaione warm or chilled, plain or with fresh fruit as desired.

VERO VENETIAN ROOTS

THE SPICE WHISPERER

VERO VENETIAN ROOTS
AT THE SMALL LUXURY HOTEL
CA' DI DIO
RIVA CA'DI'DIO
CASTELLO 2182
+39 041-098 02 38
vretreats.com

OPENING HOURS:

Tuesday to Sunday
7:00 PM – 10:00 PM
Closed on Mondays

The location of this popular fine-dining venue is truly special: just steps away from the Vaporetto stop at Arsenale, nestled within the Small Luxury Hotel Ca' di Dio. In medieval times, this historic building served as a pilgrimage station on the route to the Holy Land, later becoming a monastery and, much later, a retirement home. Today, it is a haven for gourmets and design enthusiasts. No less than Portuguese star architect Patricia Urquiola has masterfully transformed the somewhat claustrophobic monastic cells into bright, pastel-toned hotel rooms. From the moment you step inside, you sense a certain lightness, with a bold contrast between an oversized Murano chandelier, contemporary designer lamps, and stylish sofas and armchairs – a striking counterpoint to the opulence of Venetian palazzi. In addition to the chic Alechemia Bar, famous for its sensational cocktails, and the Essentia Restaurant, which offers breakfast in a lush courtyard, Vero stands out as the hotel's culinary flagship. Here, Patricia Urquiola conceived the idea of projecting vibrant gastronomic motifs onto the ceiling. Textured wallpapers, terrazzo floors, plush upholstered benches, and ergonomically designed chairs create a supreme sense of comfort. Even the smallest details are carefully considered: the female waitstaff glide effortlessly through the space in traditional Friulian slippers. In the kitchen, Luigi Lionetti, assisted by Sous Chef Gabriel Collazzo, showcases his passion for pure, intense flavors and an inspired use of spices like anise, nutmeg, cinnamon, and cumin. Dishes include a lemon-infused Risotto Riserva San Massimo with burrata, scampi, seaweed, and capers, or sea bass with fennel and citrus fruits. For meat lovers, the mountain lamb with black garlic and blood orange compote is a revelation, while eel with foie gras, Béarnaise sauce, and lemon offers a decadent experience. Those who assume Il Vero Spaghetto al Pomodoro is a simple pasta dish are in for a surprise. Its sauce – crafted from red and yellow date tomatoes, Corbarino, and Pachino varieties – delivers an explosion of flavors, making it a highlight of the four-course vegetarian menu, Vero.

Right – A discreet sign on the hotel's facade marks the entrance to the restaurant.

Below – Luigi sources ingredients at the Rialto Market and from his own herb garden.

Bottom – The stylish interiors of Vero, designed by Patricia Urquiola.

FAVORITE SPOTS OF LUIGI LIONETTI

For a great glass of wine and delicious cicchetti, my go-to is Osteria del Lovo, which serves the best Sarde in Saor in town alongside juicy steaks with Parmesan and arugula (Calle del Lovo, San Marco 4759). When I want to spend a special evening with Maria, my new love, I take her to my friend Salvatore's restaurant, Local. We particularly enjoy Spaghettone al Te Nero Lapsang Souchong con Ricci di Mare. An absolute dream!

CAPPELLETTI DI PARMIGIANO VACCHE ROSSE, TARTUFO NERO, ASTICE E IL SUO CONSOMMÉ

CAPPELLETTI WITH PARMESAN, BLACK TRUFFLE, LOBSTER, AND LOBSTER BROTH

SERVES 2
DIFFICULTY

DOUGH
6 ⅓ cups (800 g) type 00 flour
17.6 oz (500 g) egg yolks

FILLING
4 ⅓ cups (1 kg) heavy cream
12.3 oz (350 g) grated Parmigiano Reggiano (aged 36 months)
salt

LOBSTER
1 lobster

BROTH
shells from 1 lobster
1 celery root
3 carrots
1 onion
1 leek
0.7 oz (20 g) lemongrass

TO SERVE
black truffle

1 **DOUGH**
Combine the flour and egg yolks in a planetary mixer or with a hand mixer to create a smooth dough. Vacuum-seal and refrigerate overnight.

2 **FILLING**
Gently heat the heavy cream, melt in the Parmesan, season with salt, and remove from heat.

3 **LOBSTER**
Steam the lobster for 5 minutes, remove the meat, and slice it thinly. Set the shells aside for the broth.

4 **BROTH**
In a dry pan, toast the lobster shells with the vegetables. Cover with waterand reduce to a thick essence. Strain through a fine sieve.

5 **TO SERVE**
Roll out the cappelletti dough with a rolling pin and let it rest for 30 minutes. Cut the dough into rounds, place 1 teaspoon of filling in the center of each, fold into a half-moon shape, and seal the edges to form classic cappelletti.
Cook the cappelletti in plenty of broth until al dente. Serve in a deep plate, ladle over the remaining broth, arrange the lobster slices, shave black truffle on top, and serve hot.

RISTORANTE AL COVO

A HAVEN IN TIMES OF NEED

RISTORANTE AL COVO
CAMPIELLO DELLA PESCARIA
CASTELLO 3968
+39 041-522 38 12
ristorantealcovo.com

OPENING HOURS:

Friday to Tuesday
12:45 PM – 2:00 PM
and 7:30 PM – 10:00 PM
Closed on Wednesdays and Thursdays
Closed in January
and for 10 days in August

Cesare Benelli, a scion of a Tuscan family with a long tradition of running restaurants in Venice, and his wife Diane, a native Texan and the restaurant's warm and welcoming host since its opening in 1987, form a well-rehearsed duo. Their guests include many Biennale visitors, as the restaurant is within walking distance of the Giardini. Cesare is uncompromising when it comes to sourcing ingredients. He is one of the founding members of Osti in Orto, a collective of eleven restaurants that cultivate a shared vegetable garden on the island of Sant'Erasmo – a source of delight for crime novelist Donna Leon, who finds happiness in a simple plate of pasta with crisp, fresh vegetables. Cesare demonstrates his culinary creativity in his seafood dishes. A salad of mazzancolle (giant prawns) and canoce(mantis shrimp) or a tuna tartare with Balla Rossa beans are just two highlights. Regulars claim that his fritto misto is the best in town. The peak of the culinary calendar, however, falls in April, May, October, and November, when moeche – soft-shell crabs from the Venetian lagoon – appear at the Rialto fish market. During these brief windows, as they shed their shells, the crabs are at their most tender and delicate, lightly dusted with flour and pan-fried whole – an absolute delicacy. Diane is responsible for desserts, which include a chocolate cake to die for, a pear and plum tart with cinnamon grappa sauce, and a silky panna cotta with mandarin coulis. The restaurant's two intimate dining rooms are adorned with raw brick walls and artwork, while outdoor tables invite guests. Natural wines take center stage at Al Covo, sourced from healthy soils and vinified with minimal intervention. Cesare's wine cellar holds around 240 carefully selected labels. Together with their friend Flavio Franceschet, he and Diane also support Lagune nel Bicchiere – Le Vigne Ritrovate, an initiative dedicated to preserving small vineyards in the lagoon. On the island of San Michele, where Franciscan monks once cultivated vines, the association now produces around 1,500 bottles annually, which are not sold but used for promotional purposes.

Since 2013, Al Covo has had a little brother. Al Covino is an intimate spot with just six tables, helmed by Claudia Torcellan, and is a favorite among locals. Like its big brother, Al Covino also benefits from the Osti in Orto vegetable garden. Guests can enjoy delicacies such as Culatello ham with figs, tartare topped with quail egg, or one of the many tempting tramezzini – for instance, stuffed with cabbage, mayonnaise, broccoli, and capers from the island of Pantelleria. Three prix fixe menus are available, each featuring three courses: seafood, meat, or vegetarian. There's also the Lasseme Fa' menu, a surprise selection crafted by Chef Claudio, featuring two courses of his choice followed by a dessert from pastry chef Claudia Torcellan. (Calle del Pestrin, Castello 3829, open 12:00 PM – 2:30 PM and 6:00 PM – 10:30 PM, closed Tuesdays and Wednesdays alcovino.it)

Left – The rustic charm of Al Covo, with its exposed brick walls and wooden beam ceilings.

Below – Diane runs the front of house, while Cesare ensures that every dish meets his exacting standards.

CEVICHE DI LOTREGANO DI LAGUNA

CEVICHE OF GOLDEN MULLET

SERVES 4
DIFFICULTY

4 fresh golden mullet fillets
1 small carrot, diced
1 stalk celery, diced
½ Tropea onion, finely chopped
½ small bell pepper, finely chopped
½ boiled potato, finely diced
juice of 2 lemons
juice of 1 lime
¼ cup (50 ml) tomato water
pulp of ½ ripe avocado, puréed
1 tsp sea salt flakes

TO SERVE
20 coriander leaves
½ tsp chili powder
3 tbsp extra virgin olive oil

1 Arrange the fish fillets in the center of four soup plates. Top with carrot, celery, onion, bell pepper, and potato. Sprinkle with sea salt flakes and drizzle with lemon juice, lime juice, and tomato water. Spoon the avocado purée over the top and smooth it out.

2 **TO SERVE**
Garnish with coriander and chili powder, drizzle with olive oil, and let marinate for five minutes before serving cold.

MOECHE FRITTE E CARCIOFI VIOLETTI DI SANT'ERASMO

FRIED SOFT-SHELL CRABS WITH VIOLET ARTICHOKES FROM SANT'ERASMO

SERVES 1
DIFFICULTY

2 oz (60 g) Type 0 flour
1 tbsp (15 g) cornstarch
16 medium moeche (Venetian soft-shell crabs)
1 ¼ cups (300 ml) grapeseed or peanut oil
6 violet artichokes from Sant'Erasmo
Juice of 1/2 lemon
¾ cup (200 ml) cold whole milk
salt

TO SERVE
4 sprigs wild fennel

1 Mix the flour and cornstarch. Make a small incision between the eyes of the crabs, then dredge them in the flour mixture. Heat the oil to 180°C and fry the crabs for about one minute per side until golden brown. Drain on paper towels. Remove the tough outer leaves of the artichokes and trim the tops. Cut in half lengthwise, then slice into four to six wedges. Rub with lemon juice to prevent discoloration. Dip the artichoke wedges in milk, then dredge in the flour mixture. Fry in the remaining oil for one and a half minutes until crispy. Drain on paper towels and sprinkle with salt while still hot.

2 **TO SERVE**
Arrange the fried moeche and artichokes on a plate, garnish with wild fennel, and serve immediately.

OSTERIA ALLE TESTIERE

EARLY RISER

OSTERIA ALLE TESTIERE
CALLE DEL MONDO NOVO
CASTELLO 5801
+39 041/522 72 20
osterialletestiere.it

OPENING HOURS:

7:00 PM – 11:00 PM
Closed on Sundays and Mondays
Closed in August and from mid-December to mid-January

C

Chef Bruno Gavagnin is an early riser, preferring to visit the Rialto Market at dawn to select the freshest seafood before having it delivered to his small restaurant near Campo Santa Maria Formosa. The secret of his cuisine lies in the combination of fish and spices, a tradition rooted in the oldest cookbooks of the Serenissima. His creativity knows no bounds, from his signature dish of scallops sautéed in olive oil with garlic, mint, and lemon to mussels gently steamed with ginger or mini gnocchi with baby squid and a hint of cinnamon. Bruno's passion for cooking was inspired by his mother, who worked as a private chef. It was only natural that he attended culinary school and went on to work in some of Venice's most respected hotels and restaurants. His last stop before opening his own place in 1993 was Corte Sconta. While Bruno is known for his grounded and thoughtful nature, his partner, the charming sommelier Luca di Vita, is his perfect counterbalance. Since 1994, Luca has been at his side, overseeing the seamless operation of their small but mighty culinary haven, which has only eleven tables. At lunchtime, each table is used only once, but in the evening, they turn over twice due to space constraints. Every ingredient is sourced fresh daily, with just enough purchased to fit into the restaurant's modest refrigerator. This limited capacity comes with advantages – flexibility to create dishes based on what's best at the market, with no need to rely on frozen ingredients or rigid menus. Their commitment to Venetian traditions extends to cicchetti, Venice's beloved small bites. Many guests prefer to sample an array of these rather than committing to a full meal. Luca's wine cellar is equally impressive, featuring treasures like Orto di Venezia vintage 2020 from Michel Toulouze's vineyard on Sant'Erasmo. Among the spirits, you'll find a dozen varieties of grappa, rum from Guyana, and limoncello from the Amalfi Coast. Bruno and Luca take great pride in exceptional service. In a time when hospitality is often undervalued, maintaining a five-person service team for just eleven tables is a rare feat. They have been members of Buona Accoglienza for nearly twenty years, working alongside like-minded restaurateurs to counteract the effects of mass tourism while preserving Venice's culinary traditions. Their mission includes supporting small vineyards, working with local suppliers, and helping expand fruit and vegetable farms on the lagoon's islands.

Left – With only eleven tables, reservations are essential.

Below – The *cicchetti* tradition lives on at Osteria alle Testiere, and the menu remains ever flexible.

Bottom – Bruno Gavagnin prepares his dishes using only the freshest ingredients sourced from the morning's market haul.

TAGLIATA DI TONNO AI CARCIOFI VIOLETTI

TUNA TAGLIATA WITH VIOLET ARTICHOKES

SERVES 4
DIFFICULTY

4 violet artichokes
1 ½ lb (700 g) tuna, skinless and boneless
2 tbsp extra virgin olive oil
1 garlic clove
8 mint leaves
½ cup (100 ml) dry white wine
8 cherry tomatoes, halved
salt and 1 tsp pink peppercorns

TO SERVE
1 bunch parsley, chopped

1 Cut off the stems of the artichokes and remove the tough outer leaves. Slice off the top third, remove the choke, and cut the hearts lengthwise into the thinnest possible strips. Cut the tuna into 4 slices, each about 1 ½ inches thick. Heat the olive oil in a pan and sauté the garlic, mint, and artichoke strips over high heat. Remove the garlic and deglaze with white wine. Add a ladleful of water, salt, and pink peppercorns, and let simmer for about 3 minutes. The cooking liquid should not completely evaporate. Turn off the heat and add the cherry tomatoes.
Grill the tuna slices on a hot griddle for no more than 1 minute per side, then transfer them to the pan. Turn the heat back on and let cook for 1 more minute.

2 **TO SERVE**
Arrange the tuna slices with the artichokes and remaining cooking liquid, sprinkle with parsley, and serve.

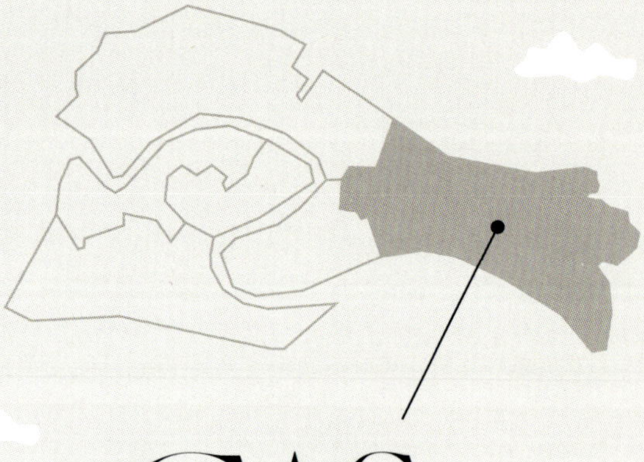

CASTELLO

1 FONDAZIONE QUERINI STAMPALIA

Until the mid-19th century, this palazzo was the residence of the noble Querini family. Today, their private art collection, featuring works by Bellini and Longhi, is a reminder of that past.

Since 1982, the library has been open to the public, with access to around 30,000 volumes in its reading room. A must-see: the garden, where architect Carlo Scarpa created a mesmerizing interplay of water and light, Murano glass tiles, trickling fountains, and the lush greenery typical of Venetian courtyard gardens. Campo Santa Maria Formosa, Castello 5252, Tel. +39 041 271 14 11, open Tuesday to Saturday from 10:00 am to 6:00 pm, closed on Mondays, ***querinistampalia.it***

2 HOTEL TIP: CASA VERARDO

Tucked away near the hidden Ponte Storto, this 16th-century palazzo is run by Daniela and Francesco Mestre. Beneath the historic wooden beams, the rooms and salons feature Fortuny lamps, Rubelli fabrics, and a mix of modern furniture and antiques. In summer, guests can relax in the patio and on the breakfast terrace. Campo SS. Filippo e Giacomo, Castello 4765, Tel. +39 041 528 61 27, double rooms from €245, ***casaverardo.it***

3 PASTICCERIA ALLA BRAGORA

One of those rare spots untouched by crowds of day-trippers, where locals stop by for a morning coffee and a cornetto on their way to work. What a lovely way to start the day. At lunchtime, it's all about toasted sandwiches, panini, and bruschetta. Later in the day, the focus shifts to sweet treats – delicate pastries, fluffy fritters, and a divine almond cake. On sunny days, the outdoor tables are a delight. Salizada S. Antonin, Castello 3604, Tel. +39 041 639 35 27, open daily from 6:30 am to 8:00 pm.

4 GIOVANNA ZANELLA

Anyone with a weakness for extravagant, eccentric shoes will not leave this store empty-handed. Giovanna Zanella, a student of renowned shoemaker Rolando Segalin, pushes creative boundaries with her designs. Handmade or even custom-made, she favors asymmetrical shapes, bold colors like red, pink, and purple, and striking details. These shoes are guaranteed to turn heads – and she even has male clients who commission understated classics tailored to their feet. Visitors can watch her work in the shop or sign up for one of her workshops. Calle Carminati, Castello 5641, Tel. +39 041 523 55 00, open from 11:30 am to 7:30 pm, closed on Sundays, ***giovannazanella.com***

5 VIZIO VIRTÙ

Even if you just stop by for a quick hot chocolate, this artisan chocolatier, lovingly run by Mariangela Penzo and Laura Bubacco since 2005, is well worth a visit. Passionate chocolate lovers will find everything their hearts desire – cakes, biscotti, pralines, and unusual chocolate varieties infused with basil, pepper, ginger, tobacco, or champagne. A great idea: workshops on traditional biscotti, chocolate, and gelato. Calle del Forner, Castello 5988, Tel. +39 041 275 01 49, open daily from 10:00 am to 7:00 pm, ***viziovirtu.com***

6 MUSEO STORICO NAVALE

Once a grain warehouse in the 16th century, today Italy's most important naval museum. Four floors display historic maritime maps, sextants, cannons, naval uniforms, ship models, and many other artifacts from Venice's time as a powerful naval force, as well as from the periods of Habsburg and Napoleonic rule. One of its highlights is the Bucintoro, the Venetian doges' opulent state barge, rowed by 168 oarsmen. Built in 1728 at the Arsenale, the city's famous shipyard, it remains a masterpiece. Riva San Biasio, Castello 2148, Tel. +39 041 244 13 99, marina.difesa.it. Extra tip: Maritime enthusiasts can stay at the nearby Hotel Bucintoro, where rooms are inspired by the officers' quarters of traditional tall ships. ***hotelbucintoro.com***

7 SERRA DEI GIARDINI

A former Art Nouveau greenhouse with an orangery, now home to a flower shop and a charming café with a garden. Located near the Vaporetto stop Giardini, it's an ideal venue for Biennale events or intimate private gatherings. Stop by for a coffee and a sandwich, browse the books and magazines, and enjoy the relaxing music. Via Giuseppe Garibaldi, Castello 1254, Tel. +39 041 296 03 60, open from 10:00 am to 8:00 pm, closed on Mondays.

LIBRERIA AQUA ALTA 8

Its location near St. Mark's Square means this beloved bookstore regularly floods when high tide rolls in. To keep his books as dry as possible, Luigi Frizzo came up with a unique solution: instead of shelves, he stores his delicate wares in waterproof barrels, old bathtubs, a canoe, and even an antique gondola. Hard to believe, but despite the apparent chaos, he knows exactly where to find anything – books, magazines, maps, whether secondhand or just published. The back room is a perfect retreat for quiet reading. Calle Longa Santa Maria Formosa, Castello 5176/B, Tel. +39 041 296 08 41, open daily from 9:00 am to 7:30 pm.

SAN POLO

9333

Pedestrian bridges over the city's many canals.

At night, the Grand Canal is eerily quiet, with only the occasional Vaporetto passing through.

SAN POLO

Only insiders understand the meaning of the many coats of arms and symbols.

With just 33 hectares, this district, named after its parish church, is the smallest in the city yet also the most densely populated. Its biggest attraction is undoubtedly the Rialto Bridge, which connects San Polo to the other side of the Grand Canal at its narrowest point of just 28 meters. That it has always been a busy crossing is evident from history: the original wooden bridge collapsed under the weight of pedestrians in 1444. It took a long time to restore what was then the only link across the city's main waterway. In the late 16th century, architect Antonio da Ponte designed a more stable arch made from durable Pietra d'Istria, ensuring that two ships could pass beneath it simultaneously. Until the 19th century, this was the only way to cross the Grand Canal on foot. The Rialto Market, a tourist attraction in its own right, is open from Monday to Saturday from 7:30 am, offering seasonal treasures from the lagoon's islands: zucchini and baby artichokes from Sant'Erasmo, strawberries and asparagus from Treporti, as well as the freshest seafood at the adjacent fish market. Nearby, small family-run shops offer cured meats, cheeses, and other delicacies. A few steps away, shaded porticoes reveal a slice of traditional Venetian life. Once,

As evening falls, outlines sharpen in the soft twilight.

Violet artichokes – one of the most belo-
ved vegetables in Venetian kitchens.

Antonio da Ponte designed the stable Rialto Bridge.

these modest wine bars were frequented by craftsmen and merchants, but today, Bacari have become popular for their authentic charm. These simple establishments offer affordab-le wines and hearty cicchetti, a perfect way for budget-con-scious visitors to experience Venetian flavors.

San Polo was Venice's birthplace, where fleeing Romans first settled to escape the barbarian invasions. Where commerce thrives, so does everything else – during the 16th century, this district was a playground for gamblers and courtesans. Today, life is much quieter in its hidden campi and campielli, where locals shop with rolling carts or walk their dogs.

A common sight: photographing the Grand Canal from the Vaporetto.

In simple taverns, locals meet for drinks and conversation.

WISTÈRIA

A FAIRYTALE DINING EXPERIENCE

WISTÈRIA
FONDAMENTA DEL FORNER
SAN POLO 2908
+39 041-524 33 73
wisteria-restaurant.com

OPENING HOURS:

Daily 7:00 PM – 9:00 PM
Friday, Saturday, and Sunday
also 12:00 PM – 1:30 PM
Closed on Wednesday
and Thursday

An old Persian fairytale, The Three Princes of Serendip, printed in Venice in the mid-16th century, inspired the hosts of this Michelin-starred restaurant to name their tasting menus Serendipity – a refined gourmet experience full of unexpected delights and happy discoveries. For Andrea Martin and Massimiliano Rossetti, this represents the essence of their journey together, which began when they were students cooking for each other. When the opportunity arose, they opened Taverna da Baffo, a brewpub with a kitchen, attracting an eclectic crowd with live music, art exhibitions, and poetry readings. Their passion for haute cuisine grew, and when they discovered a hidden house on Fondamenta del Forner, they knew they had found their place. The wild mauve-colored wisteria in the garden inspired the name of their future fine-dining restaurant: Wistèria. Opening a restaurant in 2019 was far from ideal, but the two friends persevered and were overjoyed when their hard work was rewarded with a Michelin star in November 2021. A stroke of luck was the arrival of Valerio Dallamano, whose childhood passion for cooking was sparked by watching his mother Cristina and grandmother Clementina. He later worked with Michelin-starred chefs like Vittorio Fusari, Massimiliano Alajmo, and Emanuele Scarello. His Serendipity menus feature dishes such as Grouper Brocade (grouper with coconut and green curry) and Red Mullet Toast (red mullet with almond sauce and pepper miso). The two sommeliers, Tommaso Martin and Matteo Cesaretti, have curated a wine selection that matches the high standard set by Valerio. Astonishing highlights include Trentodoc Extra Brut Bruno Lunelli Riserva for €1,800 from Ferrari Winery or Louis Roederer Champagne Cristal Brut Vinothèque for €3400 per bottle. Among the white wines, the Venissa Bianco Isola di Mazzorbo Venezia from Tenuta Venissa holds a prestigious spot, alongside the German Riesling Zeltinger Sonnenuhr Auslese from Markus Molitor on the Mosel. The red wine selection includes Amarone della Valpolicella Classico, Château Cheval Blanc, and Château Mouton Rothschild, as well as the award-winning Pinot Noir Te Wahi Central Otago from Cloudy Bay, New Zealand.

Left – A parade of cooking spoons at the Michelin-starred restaurant Wisteria.

Below – As a young boy, he watched his grandmother cook: Chef Valerio Dallamano.

Bottom – The traditional terrazzo floor catches the eye and creates a beautiful contrast with the modern furnishings.

FAVORITE SPOTS OF ANDREA AND MAX

For authentic Venice, they head to Locanda Cipriani in Torcello for its grandeur and traditional cuisine. When they want to feel at home, they visit Osteria da Fiore, a classy spot with excellent food and a family atmosphere. (Calle del Scaleter, San Polo 2202/a).

MACCHERONI DI LENTICCHIE ROSSE IN BUSERA DI TRIGLIA

RED LENTIL MACCERONI WITH RED MULLET BUSARA

SERVES 4
DIFFICULTY

WHISKY RED MULLET
⅓ cup (80 ml) white balsamic vinegar
3 tbsp (40 ml) peated Connemara whisky
1 ½ tbsp (25 ml) mirin
1 tbsp (10 g) finely chopped mild chili peppers (ideally Cayenne)
1 ½ tsp (8 g) miso paste
6 bay leaves
1 ½ tbsp (12 g) muscovado sugar
4 tsp (10 g) salt
4 red mullet fillets, skin on

BUSARA SAUCE
¾ cup (200 ml) extra virgin olive oil
4 garlic cloves, finely chopped
2 oz (60 g) basil (leaves and stems), chopped
2 mild chili peppers (ideally Cayenne), deseeded and finely chopped
3 ½ lb (1,5 kg) pixel tomatoes, coarsely chopped
9 lb (4 kg) red mullet, gutted, cleaned, and rinsed
fish bones and heads
3 ½ oz (100 g) parsley stems
¾ oz (20 g) oregano
¾ oz (20 g) coriander
¾ oz (20 g) dill
¾ oz (20 g) marjoram
¾ oz (20 g) thyme
⅔ oz (18 g) Madras curry powder
⅓ oz (9 g) turmeric
⅓ oz (9 g) Cayenne pepper
salt to taste

RED LENTIL MACCHERONI
10 oz (300 g) red lentil flour

GOA CURRY FENNEL SORBET
18 oz (500 g) fennel, peeled and coarsely chopped
18 oz (500 g) Granny Smith apples, peeled and coarsely chopped
0.2 oz (6 g) Goa curry powder
0.04 oz (1 g) turmeric paste
2 tbsp sugar syrup
2 tbsp non-alcoholic Sambuca
2 tbsp lemon juice
0.4 oz (12 g) organic lime zest
0.2 oz (5 g) fennel powder
0.3 oz (8 g) salt

TO SERVE
black/dried limes
dill

1 WHISKY RED MULLET
Blend all ingredients except the fish into a smooth paste. Let rest in the refrigerator for at least one day. Strain the marinade through a sieve and submerge the red mullet fillets in it for at least 3 hours. Remove the fillets from the marinade, pat dry, and sear skin-side down for about 3-5 minutes. Deglaze with the marinade, remove from heat, and let cool. Cut the cooled fillets into diamond shapes and set aside.

2 BUSARA SAUCE
Heat ⅓ cup olive oil in a pan. Add garlic, basil, and chili peppers and sauté for a few minutes until fragrant. Add the chopped tomatoes and cook over high heat for about 15 minutes until soft. Pass the mixture through a large sieve and set aside. In another pan, heat the remaining olive oil. Sear the red mullet and fish bones over high heat until golden brown. Remove the bones, add the strained tomatoes, and stir in the parsley stems, oregano, coriander, dill, marjoram, and thyme. Cook everything together for about 10–15 minutes. After cooking, remove the red mullet, set aside, and keep warm. Blend the remaining mixture into a smooth sauce using a Thermomix or blender. Stir in Madras curry, turmeric, and Cayenne pepper, season with salt, and gradually incorporate the remaining olive oil until the sauce achieves a smooth consistency.

3 RED LENTIL MACCHERONI
Mix the red lentil flour with 3 tbsp room temperature water and knead into a smooth dough. Wrap in plastic wrap and let rest for at least 1 hour. Feed the dough into an electric pasta machine with a maccheroni attachment and cut the resulting pasta into pieces about 1 inch long.

4 GOA CURRY FENNEL SORBET
Blend all ingredients into a smooth mixture. Pour into a Pacojet container and freeze at -6 °F for at least 24 hours, then process into a creamy sorbet.

5 TO SERVE
Crumble the dried limes with your hands and grind into a fine powder. Bring plenty of water to a boil and cook the lentil maccheroni for about 3 minutes in simmering salted water until al dente. Arrange the red mullet with the busara sauce in a deep plate. Place the lentil maccheroni next to it. Add a scoop of fennel sorbet, dust with a pinch of lime powder, and garnish with dill.

QUAGLIA ARROSTITA, CASTAGNE E CAPOLINI

ROASTED QUAIL, CHESTNUTS AND RADICCHIETTI

SERVES 20
DIFFICULTY

QUAIL LEGS IN VERDUZZO MARINADE
4 cups (1 l) Verduzzo wine from the Zof farm
⅔ cup (150 ml) honey vinegar
3 ½ oz (100 g) wildflower or acacia honey
¾ oz (20 g) thyme
¾ oz (20 g) rosemary
¾ oz (20 g) bay leaves
1 celery stalk, chopped
1 yellow onion, chopped
2 carrots, chopped
1 ½ tsp (4 g) salt
lemon pepper
8 quail legs

QUAIL BROTH
2 cups (500 g) butter
30 quail carcasses
10 bay leaves
10 sprigs thyme
5 sprigs rosemary
4 cups (1 l) Verduzzo wine
3 carrots, diced
1 celery stalk, diced
1 yellow onion, chopped
3 dried shiitake mushrooms
1 postcard-sized piece of kombu seaweed

WINE SAUCE
½ cup (100 ml) quail broth
1 ¼ oz (35 g) Verduzzo reduction
½ tsp (3 g) Cabernet reduction
1 tsp (6 g) Dijon mustard
½ tsp (3 g) sugar
¾ oz (20 g) cooked potatoes
½ tsp (3 g) salt
4 oz (115 g) butter from roasting the carcasses

MERLINO REDUCTION
8 cups (2 l) Merlino from Pojer e Sandri
1 ¾ oz (50 g) whole cane sugar

CHESTNUT PURÉE
4.4 lbs (2 kg) chestnuts
⅓ cup (100 ml) quail broth
1 oz (30 g) butter from roasting the carcasses
0.25 oz (7 g) acacia honey
½ tbsp honey vinegar
0.3 oz (9 g) salt

BLOSSOM HEADS
1 radicchio
1 garlic clove
1 tbsp olive oil
salt

1 QUAIL LEGS IN VERDUZZO MARINADE
Combine all ingredients except the quail legs and let infuse overnight. Strain the marinade and marinate the quail legs for at least 4 hours. Remove from the marinade, rinse, and pat dry. Place in a vacuum-seal bag with a drizzle of olive oil and cook sous vide at 140 °F for 8 hours. Let cool, remove from the bag, and allow to dry. Remove the leg bone.

2 QUAIL BROTH
Melt the butter in a large pot and roast the quail carcasses with bay leaves, thyme, and rosemary over high heat for a few minutes.
Strain the butter and set it aside. Return the carcasses to the hot pot and deglaze with the wine. Add the remaining ingredients, pour in 20 cups of water, and simmer for 2 hours, skimming any foam. Strain the broth through a fine sieve and reduce to 2 cups.

3 WINE SAUCE
Blend all ingredients except the butter into a smooth purée using a high-powered blender. Incorporate the butter without heat.

4 MERLINO REDUCTION
Reduce the Merlino wine and sugar over high heat until thick and syrupy.

5 CHESTNUT PURÉE
Score the chestnuts crosswise. Roast in the oven until soft, then peel and purée. Mix with broth, butter, honey, and vinegar, season with salt, and keep warm.

6 BLOOMS
Clean the blooms by removing the outer leaves and gently twisting the root. Halve and sauté in a pan with garlic, oil, and salt.

7 TO SERVE
Season the dried quail legs with salt, brush with the reserved butter, and grill briefly until golden and crispy. Loosely cover with foil and let rest. Just before serving, heat the quail legs in the oven.
Spoon the chestnut purée on the right side of the plate and place a quail leg on top. Pour the wine sauce on the left and lay another quail leg over it. Arrange the sautéed blooms over the dish and drizzle with the Merlino reduction. Serve hot.

TRATTORIA ANTICHE CARAMPANE

FAMILY-FRIENDLY

TRATTORIA ANTICHE CARAMPANE
RIO TERRA DE LE CARAMPANE
SAN POLO 1911
+39 041-524 01 65
anticchecarampane.com

OPENING HOURS:

Daily 12:30 PM – 3:00 PM
and 7:30 PM – 10:30 PM
Closed on Sundays and Mondays

It's best to set out early if you have a reservation here. Wandering through the labyrinthine alleys, it's easy to get lost – a fortunate fact, since not everyone takes the trouble. In earlier days, when this part of San Polo was known as the red-light district, the streets were bustling. Prostitution was tolerated, and women in the trade would advertise their services scantily clad at their windows. A market's proximity always means a large flow of people – workers, craftsmen, traders from outside the city. They were among the first patrons when Antiche Carampane opened in the 1980s. Then, as now, it was a family business. Nani and Guido Agopyan, whose ancestors came from Armenia, discovered this simple trattoria. Nani, a fishmonger, had connections to the best local suppliers and loved to experiment. He was one of the first in Venice to serve raw fish or invent unconventional combinations, like Caparossoli alla Savonarola, spaghetti with clams and Parmesan. The trattoria is also known for its fritto misto, which in many other Venetian restaurants is little more than tourist fare. Here, regulars pair it with chilled prosecco. After a few years, Nani and Guido's sister joined them, and since 2004, her son Francesco has been the soul of the business. Every morning, his first stop is the Rialto Market, where his grandfather once had a fish stall. "If the Rialto Market closes," his grandfather used to say, "Venice is dead." Francesco understands what he meant. There's nothing like being among the first customers in the morning, seeing the fish still flapping in their crates. On Sundays and Mondays, when the market is closed, so is his restaurant. A recipe by Francesco: Tagliatelle with vegetables from Osti in Orto on Sant'Erasmo Island and burrata cream with turmeric. To drink, guests can order Bianco delle Marche or Sauvignon dei Colli Orientali Friulani by the glass or carafe, as well as a red Merlot from Friuli or a Valpolicella from Veneto. In 2019, Francesco traveled to Armenia, the land of his ancestors, who fled Istanbul in 1915 during the genocide. A century earlier, Armenian monks had founded a monastery on one of the lagoon's islands, now known as Isola di San Lazzaro degli Armeni. In summer, Francesco sets up a few outdoor tables. Whether at lunch or dinner, the trattoria is usually packed, so reservations are a must. Those lucky enough to secure a spot might be greeted by the host with a bag of crispy lagoon crabs.

Left – The walk through the alleys of the former red-light district is worth it.

Below – The family of Francesco Agopyan originally comes from Armenia.

Bottom – Many longtime regulars from the neighborhood remain loyal to the trattoria.

SPAGHETTI IN CASSOPIPA

SPAGHETTI WITH SEAFOOD

SERVES 6
DIFFICULTY

10 oz (300 g) mussels
10 oz (300 g) garusoli (murex or sea snails)
14 oz (400 g) clams
7 oz (200 g) razor clams
olive oil
1 garlic clove
7 oz (200 g) onions, finely chopped
2 celery stalks, finely chopped
2 carrots, finely chopped
7 oz (200 g) small squid, cut into pieces
1 cup (250 ml) white wine
⅓ cup (75 ml) cognac
1 whole nutmeg
2 tsp (10 g) dried ginger
2 tsp (10 g) cinnamon
2 tsp (10 g) cardamom
2 tsp (10 g) coriander seeds
1 ½ lb (700 g) bigoli pasta
1 tbsp tomato sauce (optional)

1 Clean the shellfish thoroughly, then sauté them separately in a pan with olive oil and a garlic clove, adding half a glass of water each time. Discard any closed shells and remove the shells from the remaining shellfish. Strain the cooking liquid through a fine cloth to remove any traces of sand and set aside.

2 Heat olive oil in a terracotta pot, if possible. Add the onions, celery, and carrots and sauté slowly for about 15 minutes. Add the shellfish and squid pieces, deglaze with white wine and cognac, and toss well.

3 Heat the clam cooking liquid. Place the spices in a tea strainer or wrap them in fine muslin and add them to the broth. Reduce the heat to the lowest setting and slowly pour in the remaining shellfish broth.
Cook the pasta in plenty of boiling salted water according to the package instructions until al dente. Drain and add the sauce with the tomato sauce, if using, to a pan over high heat. Toss the pasta well with the sauce and shellfish, divide among deep plates, and drizzle with olive oil before serving.

SEPPIE IN NERO NOSTRANO CON POLENTA

SQUID IN BLACK SAUCE WITH POLENTA

SERVES 4
DIFFICULTY

1 ¾ lb (800 g) local squid, cleaned
2 cups (500 ml) sunflower oil
1 white onion, chopped
2 tbsp tomato paste
1 oz (30 g) parsley, chopped
4 squid ink sacs
3 ¼ cups (800 ml) water
¾ cup (200 ml) milk
1 tsp salt
9 oz (250 g) cornmeal (such as Polenta Biancoperla)
2 oz (50 g) butter
salt

EXTRA TIP:

The best time to enjoy fresh squid in Venice is March and April, when they migrate into the lagoon.

1 Cut the squid into 1 ½ inch pieces. Heat the sunflower oil in a pan. Add the onion, squid, tomato paste, parsley, and squid ink sacs. Cook over low heat, stirring, until the ink sacs release their color. Simmer for about 45 minutes. If necessary, season with salt only at the end.

2 Bring the water and milk to a boil in a pot. Add the salt and gradually stir in the cornmeal. Cook the polenta over low heat for 5-10 minutes, stirring frequently. Then reduce the temperature and let it rest for another 10 minutes. Stir in the butter before serving.

3 Serve the squid and black sauce with soft Polenta Biancoperla.

OSTERIA BANCOGIRO

A HOUSE WITH HISTORY

OSTERIA BANCOGIRO
CAMPO SAN GIACOMETTO
SAN POLO 122
+39 041-523 20 61
osteriabancogiro.it

OPENING HOURS:

Daily 9:00 AM – 12:00 AM
Closed on Mondays

From Ruga dei Orefici, you reach Campo San Giacomo di Rialto, home to the oldest church in Venice. The locals lovingly call it San Giacometto, as it is so small. For centuries, it has been dedicated to the patron saint of the Rialto market traders. Under the arcades that frame the square, you'll find the entrance to Bancogiro. As its name suggests, this location was once a banking institution, as well as a storage hall for citrus fruits from the Orient. The building has been renovated and now houses a few trendy bars and bistros. One of them kept the name Bancogiro. The ground floor and upper level exude history, while the interior is modern. Downstairs, a long counter displays an extensive selection of cicchetti, while upstairs, guests dine under a historic brick vault, especially in winter. But the true highlight is the large terrace directly on the Grand Canal. The tables are well-spaced, and large white umbrellas provide shade in the midday sun. The host trio – Davide, Gianluca, and Mauro – ensure their guests are well taken care of. In the kitchen, Jacopo Capponi, Jacopo Zamboni, and Andrea Masutti enjoy a unique advantage: they are just a few steps from the Rialto Market, allowing them to buy fresh ingredients at a moment's notice. In earlier times, wealthy Venetians conducted financial transactions under the arcades, settling debts and redeeming loans. Today, morning strollers and market shoppers stop by for breakfast. Sitting on the terrace, right on the Grand Canal, sipping cappuccino with cornetto or brioche, watching gondolas, vaporetti, motorboats, and cargo barges making their deliveries – it's simply priceless. By late morning, visitors order small delicacies such as Melanzane con piovra lardo, Gamberetti al curry e ricotta, Cozze e Bottarga, or Insalata tiepida di polipo, paired with one of the many excellent house wines. The main courses change daily based on the market's freshest offerings. Venetian classics are given a modern twist – scallop strudel, rabbit with curry, goat's milk, clove sauce, and artichokes, or pasta with Marsala béchamel, roasted pork belly, and peas. The desserts are all homemade, such as Il Tartufo Tartufato, a Bavarian cream with mascarpone, cocoa, honey, and black truffle.

Far left – A wide selection of cicchetti, paired with fine wines by the glass.

Left – In winter, guests dine under a historic brick vault.

Below – Visionary and culinary artist: Gianluca Guadagni and head chef Jacopo Capponi.

FAVORITE SPOTS OF DAVIDE

There are a few hidden gems on the Lido and around the lagoon that are best kept secret. But let's share just one: Chiosco Macondo at Alberoni Beach, a tiny beach bar that is hard to find. You sit under the trees, enjoying Spaghetti Vongole to the sound of '70s music.
Not much of a secret anymore is Da Celeste on the small neighboring island of Pellestrina, a top address for seafood lovers, perfect for a Sunday lunch with a breathtaking view.

VELLUTATA DI SPINACI

CREAMY SPINACH SOUP WITH PASTIN, GOAT CHEESE, AND GARLIC-CHILI CROÛTONS

SERVES 4
DIFFICULTY

28 oz (800 g) fresh spinach, cleaned
7 oz (200 g) cooked potatoes
⅔ cup (150 ml) heavy cream
5 oz (150 g) pastin (seasoned sausage meat), in pieces
1 wheat baguette, cut into ½ inch cubes
⅔ cup (150 ml) extra virgin olive oil
2 garlic cloves, chopped
2 tsp (10 g) chopped chili pepper
3 oz (80 g) goat cheese
salt

1 Blanch the spinach in boiling water for 10 minutes, drain, and cool in ice water. Place the spinach and potatoes in a pot, then purée, season with salt, and add ⅓ cup heavy cream. Warm slightly and keep warm.

2 Sauté the pastin in a hot pan, then drain the fat.

3 Meanwhile, toss the bread cubes with a mixture of olive oil, garlic, and chili, then season with salt. Spread on a baking sheet and bake at 320 °F for 15 minutes.

4 Mix the goat cheese with the remaining ⅓ cup heavy cream and transfer to a piping bag.

5 Season the spinach soup with salt and divide among four soup plates. Sprinkle with croûtons and sautéed pastin, pipe small dots of goat cheese cream on top, and serve.

SEPPIA ARROSTO

GRILLED SEPIA IN SAOR WITH BLACK FREGULA SARDA, BISQUE, AND CELERIAC

SERVES 4
DIFFICULTY

SAUCE
2 tbsp extra virgin olive oil
7 oz (200 g) white onions, finely sliced
½ cup (100 ml) white wine
1 oz (30 g) raisins
1 oz (30 g) pine nuts
½ cup (100 ml) white vinegar
salt

BISQUE
2 tbsp extra virgin olive oil
18 oz (500 g) shellfish shells
2 tomatoes, chopped
1 onion, chopped
1 celery stalk, chopped
3 carrots, chopped
2 oz (60 g) ginger, peeled

CELERIAC
1 small celeriac, peeled, cut into ¼-inch thick slices
extra virgin olive oil
salt

BLACK FREGULA
ink from 4 squid
2 oz (50 g) fregula sarda

GRILLED SEPIA
4 squid, about 4 oz (120 g) each, cleaned

1 **SAUCE**
Heat the oil in a pot and sauté the onions over medium heat. Season with salt, add white wine, raisins, and pine nuts, and let simmer for a few minutes, then add the vinegar. Cook over low heat for about 60 minutes, then set aside some onions if desired and purée the rest into a smooth sauce. Keep warm.

2 **BISQUE**
Heat the olive oil in a pot and sear the shellfish shells with the vegetables over high heat. Once everything is browned, cover with ice, add the ginger, and cook for 45 minutes. Blend everything and strain through a fine sieve. Return the bisque to the pot and let it reduce over low heat for another 45 minutes.

3 **CELERIAC**
Place the celeriac slices on a baking sheet and bake at 350 °F for 15 minutes, then brush with oil and season with salt.

4 **BLACK FREGULA**
Bring plenty of salted water to a boil, add the squid ink, and cook the fregula for 9 minutes. Drain and set aside.

5 **SEPIA**
Grill the squid on a hot griddle, fill with the black fregula, and place in a baking dish. Cook in the oven at 410 °F for 5 minutes.

6 **TO SERVE**
Divide the bisque among four deep plates. Place the celeriac slices in the center, cover with the sauce, and set the stuffed squid on top. Optionally, garnish with the reserved sautéed onions and serve immediately.

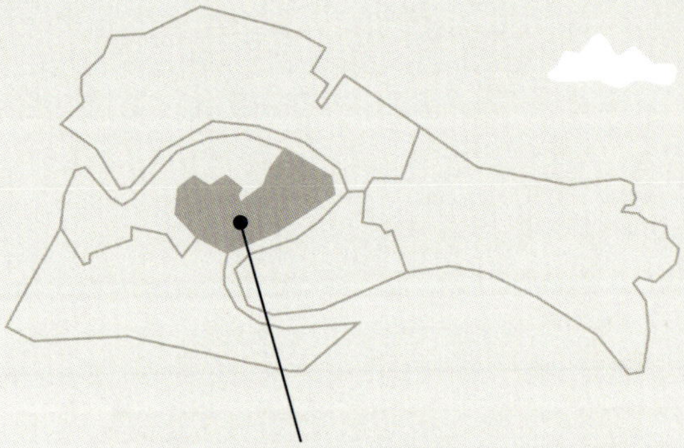

SAN POLO

1 HOTEL TIP: OLTRE IL GIARDINO

The artist and muse Anna Mahler lived here with her third husband, Franz Werfel, until 1935. The garden is an oasis, and in the patio, the air is filled with the scent of roses and lavender. The most beautiful of the six rooms in this three-story brick villa are "Turquoise" and "Green", slightly larger and more expensive than the others. ***oltreilgiardino-venezia.com***

2 ATTOMBRI

Since the late 1980s, the Attombri brothers, Stefano and Daniele, have been renowned for their modern, unique jewelry, combining antique and contemporary Murano glass beads with silver wire. Each piece is a one-of-a-kind creation, from simple rings to bold statement necklaces. Attombri has been a fixture in the fashion world, appearing in the collections of Romeo Gigli and Dolce & Gabbana. Among its loyal customers is Italian style icon and singer Antonella Ruggiero. Sotoportico di Rialto, San Polo 65, Tel. +39 041 521 25 24, open from 10:00 am to 1:00 pm and 2:30 pm to 6:30 pm, closed on Sundays, ***attombri.com***

3 PASTICCERIA RIZZARDINI

The antique lantern outside hints at the long history of this beloved pastry shop, which dates back to 1752. The selection of cookies and cakes is impressive: from Lingue di Suocera (mother-in-law's tongues) to vanilla cream-filled Millefoglie, frittelle with raisins and zabaglione cream, and the bittersweet Amaretti di Venezia.
Another classic is the Scaleteri, a delicate, wafer-thin pastry served with a cup of Caffè del Doge, a local Venetian specialty. Campiello dei Meloni, San Polo 1415, Tel. +39 041 522 38 35, open 7:00 am to 7:30 pm, closed on Tuesdays and throughout August.

4 CASA DEL PARMIGIANO

For those who can't resist shopping on the Rialto Market before heading home, this shop is unmissable. While local housewives flock here for pecorino, provolone, and fresh pasta, visitors are drawn to the house specialty of this family-run gourmet store: Parmigiano. The vacuum-sealed packaging makes it easy to take this prized cheese home. Campo Bella Vienna, San Polo 214, open Monday to Wednesday from 7:30 am to 1:30 pm and Thursday to Saturday until 7:30 pm.

5 AI NOMBOLI

From the outside, this unassuming bar might not catch the eye, but inside, it reveals itself as a true paradise for sandwich lovers. The selection is remarkable, the ingredients are of the highest quality, and special requests are always welcome. On sunny days, the outdoor seating is particularly inviting. Located near Campo San Polo, close to the home of Commissario Brunetti in Calle Dolera Attorno Brusà 1421a, where many family scenes in the films take place. Rio Tera dei Nomboli, San Polo 2717/c, Tel. +39 041 523 09 95, open Monday to Friday from 7:00 am to 9:00 pm, Saturday from 7:00 am to 3:00 pm, closed on Sundays.

6 DROGHERIA MASCARI

Truffles, dried mushrooms, cookies, chocolate, tea, and an impressive selection of exotic spices fill this tiny shop to the brim. The Mascari family runs this beloved store near the Rialto Market with passion and dedication. A hidden treasure for wine lovers can be found in the back room: over 1,000 bottles, including 600 prestigious Italian labels, such as Antinori, Masi, Sassicaia, and Brunello di Montalcino. Ruga dei Speziali, San Polo 381, Tel. +39 041 522 97 62, open from 8:00 am to 1:00 pm and from 4:00 pm to 7:30 pm, closed on Sundays and Wednesday afternoons, ***imascari.com***

7 PIEDÀTERRE

In Venice, the velvet slippers available in many places are called Friulane. Their origins date back to the 19th century, when women in the villages of Friuli began sewing shoes for their families from fabric scraps and bicycle rubber. Over time, they evolved into cult objects, refined in both form and quality, and have become particularly popular among tourists.

In 1952, the story of Piedàterre began with a handcart serving as a sales stand on the Rialto Bridge. Forty years later, the first real store was opened nearby. To this day, these elegant slippers are crafted from 100% cotton and velvet. Ruga dei Oresi, Sotoportico, San Polo 60, Tel. +39 041 850 65 74. The brand has since expanded beyond its historic store, adding a much larger flagship boutique in San Marco. Campo Santo Stefano, San Marco 2806, Tel. +39 041 319 52 91, ***piedaterrevenezia.com***

SCUOLA GRANDE DI SAN ROCCO 8

Founded in 1478, this brotherhood house, one of six in Venice, could just as well be called the Tintoretto Museum. The renowned Venetian painter left behind an extensive cycle of paintings. His first work here was dedicated to Saint Roch, the patron saint of plague victims. From 1576 to 1581, he covered the walls with large-scale depictions of Old Testament scenes. On the ground floor, visitors will find his final works, this time focusing on the New Testament. After the visit, a stop at the nearby Chiesa di San Rocco is worthwhile, where additional masterpieces by Tintorettocan be admired. Campo San Rocco, San Polo 3052, ***scuolagrandesanrocco.org***

SANTA CROCE

GENNI
ANNA

Short and to the point:
an overview of everything
there is.

Early in the morning the Grand Canal
belongs to the transport boats.

SANTA CROCE

The sestiere was named after the church that was demolished in the nineteenth century. The last remaining trace of it is a column at the Fondamenta della Croce, diagonally across from Santa Lucia train station, at the entrance to the Giardini Papadopoli, which were created in its place. Even greater transformations took place, particularly during the Habsburg era, when the canals between the many small islands were filled in. Today, the houses of the approximately five thousand residents rest on fourteen small islands, forming a total land area of ninety-four hectares. Sestiere Santa Croce largely belongs to the Venetians. Slightly removed from the usual hustle and bustle, places like Campo San Giacomo dell'Orto offer glimpses into everyday life that seem frozen in time. Neighbors exchange the latest news on benches, children play soccer, and in the small bars, people leisurely enjoy their daily apéritif. However, the sestiere has also expanded in recent years. In the 1960s, the artificially created Isola Nuova, also known as Tronchetto, was developed with a ferry and cruise terminal as well as a four-story parking garage, where even Venetians park their cars. Piazzale Roma,

Simple & elegant:
the Ponte de la Costituzione.

A popular souvenir Murano glass in all
colors and shapes.

Female gondoliers are still a minority.

A leisurely ride with little traffic on the Grand Canal.

where thousands of tourists arrive daily, has been connected to the mainland by the Ponte della Libertà since 1933. In 2008, the fourth bridge over the Grand Canal was inaugurated, the ninety-four-meter-long Ponte della Costituzione, designed by renowned Spanish architect Santiago Calatrava, made of glass and stone, linking the train station with Piazzale Roma. Another bridge, the Ponte delle Tette, which crosses the Rio San Canciano at the border to San Polo, owes its unmistakable name to the fact that in the fifteenth century, women offering their services were officially permitted to present themselves topless in an attempt to outcompete their male rivals. Whether they were successful, however, remains questionable.

Locals reading the daily newspaper *Il Gazzettino*.

Those who can afford it have their own private dock.

RISTORANTE GLAM

FINE DINING RENAISSANCE

RISTORANTE GLAM
IM PALAZZO VENART
CALLE TRON
SANTA CROCE 1961
TEL. +39 041-523 37 84
ldchotelsitaly.com

OPENING HOURS:

12:30 PM to 14:30 PM
and 19:30 PM to 22:30 PM
Closed on Monday and Tuesday

Venice's top fine dining establishments have secured their place in the Michelin Guide rankings. At present, four restaurants hold a single star – Local, Wistèria, Quadri, and Venissa – while Glam remains the city's only two-starred venue. The excellence of its cuisine is rivaled only by the extraordinary location on the ground floor of Palazzo Bacchini delle Palme. A Taiwanese investor assembled a team of architects, designers, artisans, historians, and specialists from Fondazione La Fenice to restore the sixteenth-century palace, which reopened in 2016 as the boutique hotel Palazzo Venart with just 18 rooms and suites. Among them, the Lord Byron Suite stands out with silk and brocade-covered walls, while the bathrooms are so opulent that Liberace himself would have approved. The salons, decorated with gilded frescoes, shimmering chandeliers, and a 300-year-old grand piano auctioned at Christie's, evoke a bygone grandeur. The Michelin-starred restaurant, in contrast, occupies the former orangery and presents an elegant modern aesthetic in shades of cream and caramel. With space for just 30 guests, its wide glass façade overlooks a lush courtyard, where tables are set beneath the shade of a magnolia tree in the summer. This exquisite setting is the perfect stage for Enrico Bartolini, one of Italy's most celebrated chefs, who has redefined contemporary gastronomy with his concept of a Fine Dining Renaissance. No other chef combines traditional knowledge with innovative techniques and a masterful play of flavors as he does. Of his nine top-tier restaurants in Italy and three more in Dubai, Hong Kong, and Bali, his two-starred establishment on the third floor of Milan's MUDEC Museum is widely considered his crown jewel. For his Venetian project, he was advised by Irina Freguia, an industry veteran and owner of the iconic Vecio Fritolin in Calle della Regina, who guided him through the city's finest markets and introduced him to Michele Savognano on Giudecca, where he discovered organic vegetables, rare heirloom fruit varieties, and edible flowers. His executive chef in Venice, Donato Ascani, is equally captivated by the city. "Venice is a dream for any chef," he says. "The number of vegetable gardens and vibrant markets is extraordinary, and what arrives from the sea each day is always a surprise." With such ingredients at his disposal, he approaches his menus with a sense of instinct, precision, and creativity. Guests can choose between two tasting menus, Glam's Classics and Art, Gardens, and Lagoon, or select at least three courses à la carte. Each dish is a masterpiece both in flavor and in presentation – a visual spectacle as much as a culinary delight. The soft-shell crab, served with artichokes and pink sauce, or risotto infused with Gorgonzola and beetroot, offers a symphony of color on the plate.

Left – Donato Ascani is amazed by the culinary treasures Venice has to offer.

Right – The elegant copper cookware reflects the restaurant's refined level of cuisine.

Below – The hand-selected brigade of the two-starred restaurant in action.

ACQUADELLE IN SALSA

ACQUADELLE IN SAUCE

SERVES 4
DIFFICULTY

CARPIONE
2 cups (500 ml) water
2 cups (500 ml) white vinegar
2 cups (500 ml) white wine
½ cup (100 g) sugar
1½ tbsp (40 g) salt
1 garlic clove
¼ cup (20 g) fresh thyme
1 cinnamon stick
2 tsp (10 g) black peppercorns
¼ tsp (1 g) agar-agar

PRESERVED LEMONS
¾ cup (150 g) coarse salt
⅔ cup (130 g) sugar
10 organic lemons

BLACK BÉARNAISE
3 ½ oz (100 g) egg whites
¼ cup (60 ml) grapeseed oil
1 tbsp (20 g) wine reduction
2 tsp (10 g) squid ink

PONZU SOY SAUCE
¾ cup (200 ml) ponzu sauce
2 tbsp (30 g) soy sauce
2 tsp (10 g) dashi broth
1 tsp (5 g) yuzu juice
1 ½ tsp (8 g) cornstarch

TEMPURA BATTER
1 ½ cups (200 g) rice flour
½ cup (100 g) polenta flour
⅓ cup (50 g) cornstarch
¾ tsp (2 g) bay leaf powder
¾ tsp (2 g) mustard powder
1 tbsp squid ink
3 ½ oz (100 g) acquadelle

1 **CARPIONE**
Bring water, vinegar, and wine to a boil. Add sugar, salt, garlic, thyme, cinnamon, and peppercorns. Let the mixture infuse for 12 hours, then strain. Set aside ½ cup, bring to a boil with agar-agar, and allow to cool.

2 **PRESERVED LEMONS**
Place the lemons with salt and sugar in a vacuum-seal bag. Seal and cook sous-vide at 185°F for four hours. Remove the lemons, purée the peel, and strain through a fine sieve. Transfer to a piping bag.

3 **BLACK BÉARNAISE**
Whip the egg whites, slowly incorporating the grapeseed oil. Mix in the wine reduction and squid ink until smooth. Transfer to a piping bag.

4 **PONZU SOY SAUCE**
Combine ponzu sauce, soy sauce, dashi broth, and yuzu juice. Gradually add the cornstarch while stirring continuously. Transfer to a piping bag.

5 **TEMPURA BATTER**
Mix the rice flour, polenta flour, and cornstarch. Divide into three bowls. Add ¼ cup of water to each. Stir bay leaf powder into the first, mustard powder into the second, and squid ink into the third. Divide the acquadelle evenly among the batters.
Heat oil to 350°F and fry the fish until crisp and golden. Remove with a slotted spoon and drain on paper towels.

6 **TO SERVE**
Arrange the fried acquadelle on a plate. Garnish with ponzu soy sauce, black Béarnaise, preserved lemons, and carpione marinade. For a refined finish, decorate with fresh herbs and edible flowers.

SEPPIA ALLA BRACE

GRILLED CUTTLEFISH WITH CUTTLEFISH SAUCE AND BLACK SAUCE

SERVES 4
DIFFICULTY

CUTTLEFISH SAUCE
3 ½ oz (100 g) cuttlefish trimmings
1 ¾ oz (50 g) cuttlefish innards
grapeseed oil as needed
2 cups (500 ml) soy milk
2 bay leaves

BLACK SAUCE
3 egg whites
1 oz (30 g) wine reduction
2 ¾ oz (80 g) grapeseed oil
¾ oz (20 g) cuttlefish ink
1 tsp Tabasco

GRILLED CUTTLEFISH
1 tbsp extra virgin olive oil
4 medium cuttlefish, cleaned

1 CUTTLEFISH SAUCE
Sauté the cuttlefish trimmings and innards in a saucepan over medium heat with a little grapeseed oil until browned. Deglaze with soy milk, add the bay leaves, and let the mixture simmer on low heat for 30 minutes. Strain through a fine sieve and let the liquid cool. Whisk or blend with a hand mixer, adding a little grapeseed oil, until smooth.

2 BLACK SAUCE
In a clean bowl, beat the egg whites until stiff. Slowly drizzle in the wine reduction while continuing to whisk. Gradually incorporate the grapeseed oil in a steady stream, whisking constantly until the mixture emulsifies. Fold in the cuttlefish ink and Tabasco, stirring until fully combined. Transfer to a piping bag if desired.

3 GRILLED CUTTLEFISH
Heat a grill pan over medium-high heat and add the olive oil. Place the cuttlefish on the hot grill and cook for about 1minute on each side. Depending on size, grill for another 2–3 minutes until fully cooked and marked with grill lines.

4 TO SERVE
Arrange the grilled cuttlefish on plates. Drizzle generously with the cuttlefish sauce and garnish with the black sauce, creating decorative dots or lines around the plate. Optionally, finish with fresh herbs or edible flowers.

Right – Giovanni Rigoni honed his craft under Italy's top chefs.

Far right – Lagoon vegetables are preserved using age-old techniques.

Below – A sleek, modern ambiance inside a historic tavern.

FAVORITE SPOTS OF GIOVANNI RIGONI

For Sunday lunch, the Osteria Al Cicchetto in Calle de la Misericordia is my go-to spot. The place is simple, the food is honest and good – just the way I like it (Cannaregio 367/a). Osteria Giorgione Da Masa is an entirely different experience. Each time I visit, Masahiro Homma from Yokohama surprises me with his refined Italian-Japanese fusion dishes (osteriagiorgionedamasa.com).

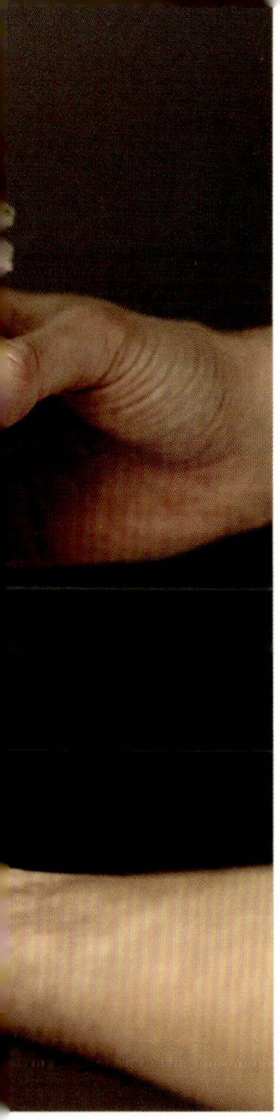

OSTERIA ZANZE XVI

TRADITION AND MODERNITY

OSTERIA ZANZE XVI
FONDAMENTA DEI TOLENTINI
SANTA CROCE 231
TEL. +39 041-71 53 94
zanze.it

OPENING HOURS:

12:00 AM to 14:00 AM
and 19:30 AM to 22:00 AM
Closed Monday and Tuesday

Not far from the train station and Piazzale Roma, a modest tavern stood here as early as the 16th century, where merchants and locals would gather at communal tables. Back then, it was known as Trattoria della Zanze, named after its first owner. A few years ago, two friends decided to revive its gastronomic past – on a much higher level. When Nicola Pasagnolo, an expert in digital strategies for the food industry, and his friend Nicola Dinato, whose culinary résumé includes the Michelin-starred Feva in Castelfranco, embarked on their project in 2017, they honored its historical roots by adding XVI to the name of their contemporary osteria. Dinato, once a pastry chef at Venice's famed Ristorante Da Fiore, gained experience with legendary chefs such as Michel Roux, Alain Ducasse, and David Bouley. During the renovation of Zanze, they preserved the original wooden beam ceilings, exposed brick walls, and marble floors. In 2021, after five years in operation, the restaurant earned a Michelin star – albeit briefly – perhaps due to its appearance on Alessandro Borghese's popular TV show 4 Ristoranti. Dinato's right-hand man in the kitchen is Giovanni Rigoni, a perfectionist whose attention to detail was shaped during seven years under Massimo Alajmo at the Michelin three-starred Le Calandre. He later worked alongside Aimo and Nadia Moroni at Bistrot Voce and spent a year as sous-chef at Feva, where he was able to experiment intensively with new recipes and techniques. Under Dinato's mentorship, he developed a deep respect for traditional Italian home cooking, emphasizing only the finest and freshest ingredients. The result is what he calls an accessible osteria with the refinement of haute cuisine. The five-course Taste of Venice menu offers an authentic take on traditional Venetian cuisine with a modern twist, while the seven-course Anima menu is a surprise selection based on the freshest market ingredients of the day.

ANGUILLA ALLA BRACE

GRILLED EEL

SERVES 2
DIFFICULTY

GRILLED EEL WITH MISO GLAZE
2 pieces of eel (each about 7–9 oz, 200-250 g)
4 tbsp light miso glaze
1 tsp vinegar powder

SEASONINGS AND SIDES
0.4 oz (12 g) rue
0.35 oz (10 g) carrot greens
1 tbsp mild vinegar marinade
1 small onion
3.5 oz (100 g) corn
1 tbsp olive oil
1 tsp green Sichuan pepper

TO SERVE
3.5 oz (100 g) mixed salad greens
3.5 oz (100 g) corn polenta
oil for frying
salt & pepper to taste

1 EEL
Brush the eel pieces with 2 tbsp of the miso glaze. Slowly grill the eel over medium heat, basting with the remaining miso glaze every 5 minutes to keep the fish moist. Cooking time varies depending on the thickness of the pieces, approximately 15-20 minutes. Lightly dust with vinegar powder just before serving.

2 SEASONINGS
Wash and dry the rue. Marinate the carrot greens with the vinegar marinade. Finely chop the onion and sauté with the corn in 1 tbsp olive oil until soft. Season with salt and pepper.

3 SIDES
Arrange the mixed salad greens and serve with a light vinaigrette. Cut the corn polenta into small pieces and fry in hot oil until golden brown. Season with salt.

4 TO SERVE
Arrange the grilled eel pieces on a plate. Garnish with the prepared rue, marinated carrot greens, and the onion-corn mixture. Sprinkle with green Sichuan pepper and serve with the salad and polenta.

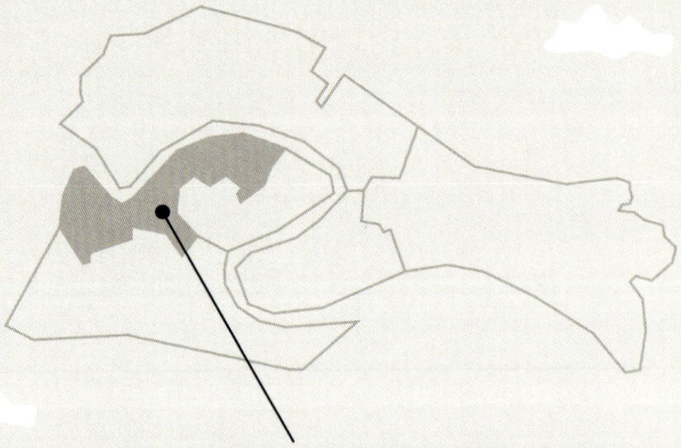

SANTA CROCE

1 HOTEL PAPADOPOLI VENEZIA MGALLERY

Nestled in the park of the same name, near Santa Lucia train station, this hotel offers rooms and suites furnished in 18th-century Venetian style, modern comforts, and a restaurant with a winter garden serving Venetian cuisine. Private boat dock available. Double rooms from €280, ***accor.com***

3 AL NONO RISORTO

Charcoal ovens, they say, are banned in Venice due to fire hazards, but that doesn't mean you can't enjoy a pizza now and then. This simple osteria features a romantically greened courtyard and an extensive menu, including Venetian specialties like sarde in saor or baccalà. Sotoportego de Siora Bettina, Santa Croce 2338, Tel. +39 041 524 11 69, open 12:00 PM – 3:00 PM and 6:00 PM – 11:00 PM, closed Wednesdays, open daily in summer from 12:00 PM – 11:00 PM.

2 PALAZZO MOCENIGO

Count Alvise Nicolò Mocenigo, the last of his line, bequeathed this five-story palazzo to the city in 1945. The house has a storied past – its most famous tenant was Lord Byron, who moved in during May 1818. Visitors can explore the richly furnished piano nobile rooms to glimpse how the 18th-century Venetian elite lived. Since the mid-1980s, it has housed Venice's Institute of Textiles and Fashion. A must-see: the perfume museum, inaugurated by interior design icon Pier Luigi Pizzi. Salizada San Stae, Santa Croce 1992, Tel. +39 041 72 17 98, open 11:00 AM – 5:00 PM, closed Mondays and Wednesdays, ***mocenigo.visitmuve.it***

4 HOTEL TIP: CA' NIGRA LAGOON RESORT

The same architect who designed the Excelsior Palace on the Lido, Giovanni Sardi, also planned this former residence of Italian ambassador Constantino Nigra. Today, it is a charming boutique hotel with 22 rooms, two lovely gardens, and a bar, conveniently located near Santa Lucia train station. Breakfast is simple, and the service is attentive. Campiello San Simeon Grande, Santa Croce 927, Tel. +39 041 524 27 90, double rooms from €270, ***hotelcanigra.com***

7 HOSTARIA VECIO BIAVEROL

This deli, overflowing with culinary delights, is a favorite among locals. Many come for the farmhouse bread with Parma ham and horseradish, while others love the Puppa Burger, named after the owner, as well as the extensive selection of creatively topped sandwiches. And, of course, there's wine, beer, and spritz. Fondamenta dei Tolentini, Santa Croce 225, Tel. +39 041 546 31 73, open Mon–Thu 11:00 AM – 2:30 PM and 5:30 PM – 9:30 PM, Fri 10:00 AM – 2:30 PM and 5:30 PM – 10:00 PM, Sat 11:00 AM – 2:30 PM and 5:30 PM – 10:00 PM, Sun 10:00 AM – 2:30 PM and 5:30 PM – 9:00 PM.

5 GELATERIA ALASKA

Under its blue-and-white-striped awning, this tiny gelateria exudes a Caribbean vibe. Carlo Pistacchi loves reggae, bright colors, and never tires of experimenting with new gelato flavors – ginger, artichoke, cinnamon, celery, or arugula. Of course, he also offers the classic creamy, fruity, and vegan varieties. Calle Larga dei Bari, Santa Croce 1159, open daily 10:00 AM – 7:30 PM.

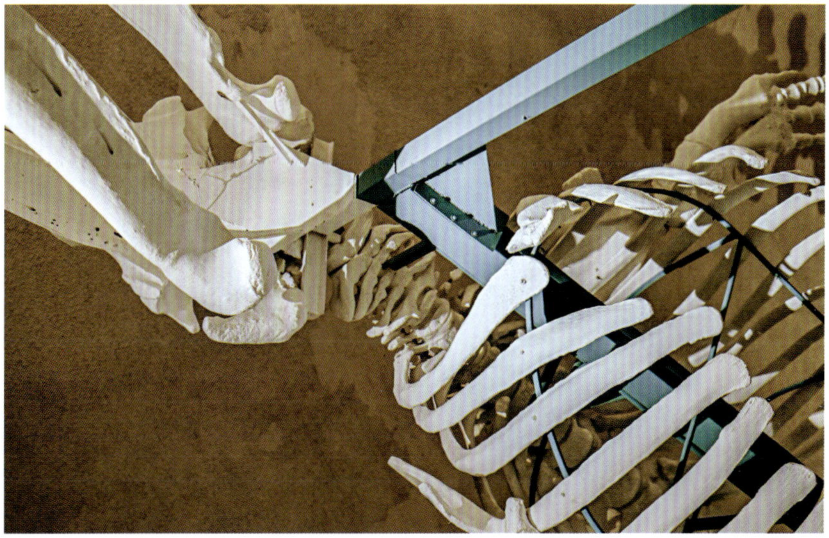

MUSEO DI STORIA NATURALE 8

Originally home to the merchant family Pesaro and later the Dukes of Ferrara, this grand palazzo on the Grand Canal became a warehouse and trading hub for Turkish merchants in 1621. Since 1923, it has housed Venice's Natural History Museum. A highlight is the dinosaur skeleton discovered in 1973 by Venetian naturalist Giancarlo Ligabue. On the ground floor, a five-meter-long aquarium represents the Adriatic's marine life at the entrance to the lagoon. In 2011, the museum underwent a thorough modernization, and today, interactive installations help illustrate scientific concepts. Salizada del Fontego dei Turchi, Santa Croce 1730, Tel. +39 041 270 03 03, open June–October Tue–Sun 10:00 AM – 6:00 PM, November – May Tue–Fri 9:00 AM–5:00 PM, Sat–Sun 10:00 AM – 6:00 PM, ***msn.visitmuve.it***

6 CA'PESARO

The wealthy Venetian Pesaro family had the means in the 17th century to build this imposing Baroque palace on the Grand Canal. Its last owner, Princess Felicita Bevilacqua La Masa, bequeathed it to the city of Venice with the stipulation that it be used for a permanent exhibition of modern art and to support young, underprivileged artists. Today, its grand halls feature works by Auguste Rodin, Egon Schiele, Marc Chagall, and Pierre Bonnard. In 2017, the private collection of Chiara and Francesco Carraro found a home here, including unique furniture by Carlo Bugatti and Eugenio Quarti and masterful Murano glassworks by Vittorio Zecchin, Seguso, and Carlo Scarpa. Also noteworthy: the Museum of Oriental Art on the third floor. Fondamenta de Ca' Pesaro, Santa Croce 2076, Tel. +39 041 72 11 27, ***capesaro.visitmuve.it***

197
198

CANNAREGIO

In the maze of working-class homes, little space remains for greenery.

Red, rust, and rose tones – colors that have inspired painters.

CANNA-REGIO

Frescoes and portals serve as ideal resting places for Venice's growing bird population.

After Castello, Cannaregio is the second-largest sestiere in Venice in terms of area. Located in the far north, it is built on 33 islands and crisscrossed by numerous small and large canals. Walking along Strada Nova, the main thoroughfare connecting the train station and Rialto Bridge, alongside thousands of tourists each day, can give a misleading impression. Cannaregio is, above all, a quiet residential and commercial district where locals still feel at home, shop, take their children to school, and meet friends on weekends in the many small bars and taverns. They tend to gather along the two long waterfront promenades, Fondamenta della Misericordia and Fondamenta Ormesini, or in the maze of narrow alleys branching off both sides of the canals, where visitors can easily get lost. When that happens, the only help is Google Maps or using Strada Nova as a pedestrian guide.

In Cannaregio, aside from Palazzo Ca' D'Oro and Palazzo Vendramin Calergi, there are fewer opulent buildings than in other parts of the city, fewer newcomers, fewer tourist shops, and fewer tourist traps. Among its many hidden squares, Campo dei Mori is particularly beloved, easily recognized by its three striking marble statues and known

At night, the city belongs to Venetians.

Gondoliers demonstrate remarkable skill navigating narrow canals.

Berths for boats are scarce in every sestiere.

as the birthplace of Tintoretto. Here, in the far north where Venice meets the lagoon, the Grand Canal comes to an end, winding its way up in an S-shape from St. Mark's Basin. The Fondamenta Nuove vaporetto station connects to the northern lagoon islands, while the cemetery island of San Michele, visible from the shore, still administratively belongs to Cannaregio. Since the 19th century, this cemetery has become the resting place of notable figures such as Igor Stravinsky and Ezra Pound. To create more burial space, additional land was reclaimed, and in 1998, star architect David Chipperfield was commissioned to design new buildings. The project began in 2004, and today, the cemetery complex includes a large hall, a chapel, and an additional crematorium.

Signs of decay: damp, crumbling masonry everywhere.

Losing your way is the best way to discover something new.

IL GIARDINO SEGRETO

ROMANTIC MOMENTS IN THE PARK

**RISTORANTE
IL GIARDINO SEGRETO
AT NH COLLECTION VENEZIA
GRAND HOTEL PALAZZO DEI
DOGI
FONDAMENTA MADONNA
DELL'ORTO
CANNAREGIO 3500
TEL. +39 041 220 88 10**
nh-hotels.com

OPENING HOURS:

7:00 AM - 11:00 AM
and 7:00 PM - 10:30 PM

Once past the train station, an untouched slice of everyday Venice begins. Workers and artisans come and go, stepping on and off the vaporettos. At the Madonna dell'Orto vaporetto stop, where the ride ends, the NH Collection Ca'del Dio hotel's private dock extends into the water. From here, a shuttle departs five times daily, ferrying guests to St. Mark's Square, where they can continue their sightseeing. The row of buildings in the background appears somewhat forbidding, partly enclosed by high walls – perhaps a protective barrier against the powerful waves of the lagoon, which is so wide here that large ships use it as a channel. At the other end of the dock, a path leads into the lush botanical garden of this exclusive, secluded hideaway. Locals know the imposing 17th-century building as Palazzo Rizzi Patarol. Its first owner, the natural scientist and botanist Lorenzo Patarol, spent two years filling the 3,000-square-meter garden with rare plants from around the world. Later, the palazzo served as a monastery and then as an embassy for France and Savoy. Like many grand Venetian palazzi, this one also included a warehouse, meaning that the hotel's rooms and salons are spacious and airy. Famous guests who have wandered these gardens include Sharon Stone, Angelina Jolie, and even the Dalai Lama. Today, hotel guests lounge here in the sun by day, and in the evening, both visitors and locals gather at the elegantly set tables of Ristorante Il Giardino Secreto. The fine-dining kitchen is helmed by Umberto Ungaro, who, after traveling the world – including stints in Sydney, Bermuda, and Gstaad – returned to Italy to work in Puglia and later in Venice at the Hotel Europa & Regina. For the past six years, he has been the executive chef at Il Giardino Secreto, remaining true to his philosophy: sourcing the freshest ingredients from the local market and the lagoon to create modern Venetian cuisine. Signature dishes include Filetto di Manzo, beef fillet in Amarone jus with foie gras, green apple, and potato foam, or Pesce Crudo dei Dogi, marinated scampi, scallops, and salmon with avocado and fresh herbs. For dessert, he serves yogurt ice cream with warm fruit, delicately scented with coriander seeds.

Far left – The magnificent Murano chandelier dominates the lounge at Palazzo dei Dogi.

Left – Umberto Ungaro returned home after traveling the world.

Below – Romantic atmosphere along Fondamenta Madonna dell'Orto.

FAVORITE SPOTS OF UMBERTO UNGARO

For a romantic dinner, Osteria di Santa Marina is perfect, where candlelit garden seating sets the mood for delicate dishes like sweet-and-sour scallop carpaccio (osteriadisantamarina.com). And then there's my good friend Giancarlo Bellino at Antinoo's Lounge Restaurant in Hotel Centurion Palace in Dorsoduro. We used to work together at Hotel Europa & Regina, and his dishes unmistakably reflect his Apulian roots (sinahotels.com).

SPAGHETTI AGLIO, OLIO E PEPERONCINO CON COZZE, LIME E POLVERE DI PEPERONE CRUSCO

SPAGHETTI AGLIO E OLIO WITH MUSSELS, LIME, AND CRUSCO PEPPER

SERVES 2
DIFFICULTY

7 tbsp extra virgin olive oil
2 garlic cloves
3.3 lbs (1,5 kg) mussels, cleaned
2 tbsp chopped parsley
juice of 2 limes
11 oz (320 g) spaghetti
1.8 oz (50 g) finely chopped crusco pepper
black pepper

1 Heat the olive oil with one garlic clove in a large pot, then remove the garlic. Add the mussels and sear over high heat for 2-3 minutes. Add the parsley, the second garlic clove, and lime juice, then cook for another 1-2 minutes.

2 Bring a large pot of salted water to a boil and cook the spaghetti until very al dente, about 2-3 minutes less than the package instructions. Meanwhile, discard any closed mussels and remove the shells. Drain the spaghetti and add them to the pan with the mussels. Toss constantly until the pasta is fully cooked, then sprinkle with crusco pepper and black pepper. Serve hot.

FILETTO DI BRANZINO GRATINATO ALLA MEDITERRANEA CON CIME DI RAPA STUFATE E KATSUOBUSHI

MEDITERRANEAN-STYLE CRUSTED SEA BASS WITH BRAISED RAPINI AND KATSUOBUSHI

SERVES 2
DIFFICULTY

CRUST
1.8 oz (50 g) finely chopped sun-dried tomatoes
0.2 oz (5 g) finely chopped capers
0.4 oz (10 g) finely chopped pitted olives
7 oz (200 g) soft butter
1.8 oz (50 g) breadcrumbs
0.7 oz (20 g) Parmigiano Reggiano

RAPINI
2 tbsp olive oil
1 garlic clove, crushed
3 anchovies
10.5 oz (300 g) rapini

SEA BASS
1.3 lbs (600 g) sea bass fillets
2 tbsp olive oil
salt & pepper

TO SERVE
katsuobushi (dried and smoked bonito flakes)

1 **CRUST**
Mix all the crust ingredients thoroughly. Shape the mixture into a roll using plastic wrap and freeze. Remove from the plastic wrap before use and slice into 0.2-inch-thick rounds.

2 **RAPINI**
Heat the olive oil in a pan. Sauté the garlic and anchovies briefly, then add the rapini. Cover and steam for about 5 minutes.

3 **SEA BASS**
Season the sea bass fillets lightly with salt and pepper. In an ovenproof pan, sear them for 1 minute on each side in hot olive oil. Top with the still-frozen crust and place the pan in a preheated oven at 400°F for about 7 minutes.

4 **TO SERVE**
Divide the braised rapini between two plates, place the gratinéed sea bass fillets on top, and sprinkle with a small handful of katsuobushi. Serve immediately.

FILETTO DI BRANZINO GRATINATO ALLA MEDITERRANEA CON CIME DI RAPA STUFATE E KATSUOBUSHI

MEDITERRANEAN-STYLE CRUSTED SEA BASS WITH BRAISED RAPINI AND KATSUOBUSHI

SERVES 2
DIFFICULTY

CRUST
1.8 oz (50 g) finely chopped sun-dried tomatoes
0.2 oz (5 g) finely chopped capers
0.4 oz (10 g) finely chopped pitted olives
7 oz (200 g) soft butter
1.8 oz (50 g) breadcrumbs
0.7 oz (20 g) Parmigiano Reggiano

RAPINI
2 tbsp olive oil
1 garlic clove, crushed
3 anchovies
10.5 oz (300 g) rapini

SEA BASS
1.3 lbs (600 g) sea bass fillets
2 tbsp olive oil
salt & pepper

TO SERVE
katsuobushi (dried and smoked bonito flakes)

1 **CRUST**
Mix all the crust ingredients thoroughly. Shape the mixture into a roll using plastic wrap and freeze. Remove from the plastic wrap before use and slice into 0.2-inch-thick rounds.

2 **RAPINI**
Heat the olive oil in a pan. Sauté the garlic and anchovies briefly, then add the rapini. Cover and steam for about 5 minutes.

3 **SEA BASS**
Season the sea bass fillets lightly with salt and pepper. In an ovenproof pan, sear them for 1 minute on each side in hot olive oil. Top with the still-frozen crust and place the pan in a preheated oven at 400°F for about 7 minutes.

4 **TO SERVE**
Divide the braised rapini between two plates, place the gratinéed sea bass fillets on top, and sprinkle with a small handful of katsuobushi. Serve immediately.

VENICE M'ART

A CELEBRATION OF POSTVENEZIANITÀ

VENICE M'ART
AT VENICE VENICE HOTEL
CANNAREGIO 5631
TEL. +39 041-097 03 00
venicevenice.com

OPENING HOURS:

Daily from 7:00 AM
to midnight

Palazzo Ca' de Mosto, the building with the oldest stone facade in Venice, stands on the Grand Canal, diagonally across from the Rialto Market. Its Byzantine style embodies 13th-century Venetian architecture. For centuries, under the protective arch of the Sotoportego del Traghetto – its rough brick vault serving as a passageway between the inner courtyard and the water – merchants and buyers met on market days to negotiate their deals. This inspired designer duo Alessandro and Francesca Gallo to transform the expansive, open space into a concept store, art gallery, café, wine bar, and all-day dining bistro as part of their Venice M'Art project. But turning the long-abandoned palazzo into their dream property was no easy feat. Best known for their fashion label Golden Goose, famous for its high-end Italian-made cult sneakers, the Gallos spent five years planning, restoring, curating artworks, and commissioning custom furniture before finally opening Venice Venice Hotel in 2022. While the historic structure remains intact, a forward-thinking spirit flows through every room. The Gallos call their vision "Postvenezianità", an ambitious balance between historic Venice and cutting-edge contemporary innovation. With art consultant Bianca Bonaldi guiding the placement of artworks, each of the 45 rooms became a meticulously curated masterpiece. Even the treatment rooms in the Felix Anima Spa resemble modern art installations. A key element of this avant-garde concept is the Venice M'Art all-day dining venue. As throughout the hotel, art and craftsmanship seamlessly blend. Morning begins with breakfast served from a trolley, where guests can indulge in waffles, fresh fruit, Eggs Benedict, and lobster rolls at impeccably set white-clothed tables. Lunch features Cicchetti at their finest or delicate carpaccios of meat and fish, often shared in true food-sharing style. By evening, candlelight and soft music transform the terrace into a romantic haven. From 7 PM onwards, guests can enjoy duck ragù gnocchi, beef filet alla Rossini, or market-fresh vegetarian dishes such as grilled vegetables with hummus. For dessert? Perhaps an apricot soup with almond sorbet. For special events and private gatherings, the management offers exclusive use of the rooftop terrace and the Venice Bitter Club.

Left – Romantic dinner for two above the rooftops of the city.

Below – Thoughtful design concept down to the finest detail.

Bottom – Modern aesthetics meet a classic Fortuny lamp.

FRITTELLE VENEZIANE

VENETIAN FRIED DOUGH BALLS

SERVES 2
DIFFICULTY

7 oz (200 g) raisins
½ cup (125 ml) milk
1.8 oz (50 g) sugar
0.9 oz (25 g) brewer's yeast
14 oz (400 g) Type 00 flour
seeds of 1 vanilla pod
2 eggs
1.4 oz (40 g) melted butter
zest of 1 organic lemon
1 tbsp pine nuts
4 cups (1 l) peanut oil
powdered sugar

1 Soak the raisins in warm water for 10 minutes, then drain and pat dry. Warm the milk slightly with 1 tsp sugar and dissolve the brewer's yeast in it. Mix in the flour and vanilla seeds.
In a separate bowl, beat the eggs with the remaining sugar. Combine with the milk-flour mixture, butter, 4.2 fl oz water, lemon zest, pine nuts, and raisins to form a smooth dough. Cover and let rise in a warm place for 2 hours.
Heat the peanut oil in a deep stainless steel pot. Using a spoon, scoop small portions of dough, shape them into balls, and fry in batches until golden brown. Remove and drain on absorbent paper. Dust with powdered sugar and serve hot.

FEGATO ALLA VENEZIANA

VENETIAN-STYLE LIVER

SERVES 4
DIFFICULTY

1.3 lbs (600 g) calf's liver
14 oz (400 g) onions
extra virgin olive oil
0.4 oz (10 g) butter
1 tbsp (15 ml) white vinegar

1 Preheat the oven to 175°F. Clean the calf's liver thoroughly and cut into four 5.3 oz portions. Peel and finely chop the onions.

2 Heat olive oil in a pan and sauté the onions over medium heat until translucent. The onions should not brown.
In a separate pan, melt the butter and sear the calf's liver slices on all sides over high heat.

3 Transfer the liver to the preheated oven and let it cook gently for about 7 minutes. Slice the liver, mix with the sautéed onions, and deglaze the pan with a splash of white vinegar.

4 Season with freshly ground black pepper and serve immediately.

MENU

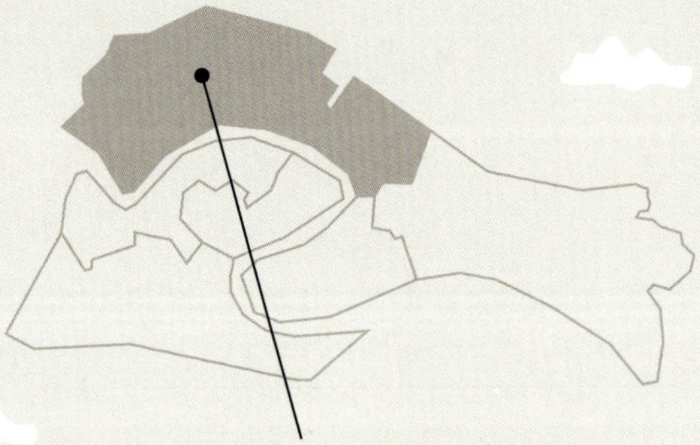

CANNA-REGIO

1 CHIESA DELLA MADONNA DEL'ORTO

A must-visit for Tintoretto enthusiasts, this historic church holds the final resting place of the great Venetian painter and his family in the choir chapel. Surrounding the altar and throughout the chapel, ten large-scale paintings bear his signature, including The Last Judgment, The Presentation of the Virgin in the Temple, and The Worship of the Golden Calf. Just steps away stands the house where Tintoretto lived for the last 20 years of his life until his death in 1594. Fondamenta della Madonna dell'Orto, Cannaregio 3512, Tel. +39 041 79 59 91

2 SULLALUNA

Francesca and Rudolfo may not be the last in a long line of dreamers to open a bookshop in Venice, but theirs stands out. Part bookshop, part bar, it offers a large selection of teas, hot chocolate, organic wines, and cider, alongside carrot and almond cakes, sandwiches, and crostini. Fondamenta della Misericordia, Cannaregio 2535, Tel. +39 041 72 29 24, open Sunday to Thursday from 9:00 AM to 9:00 PM, Friday and Saturday from 9:00 AM to 10:00 PM, ***sullalunavenezia.***

3 CASINO MUNICIPALE

Few casinos anywhere in the world can boast such an elegant setting as the Palazzo Vendramin Calergi, right on the Grand Canal. Those who can afford it arrive in style by water taxi or gondola. Venetians have always had a passion for gambling – despite frequent bans with severe penalties, there were still 136 gambling houses in the city by 1775. Strada Nova, Calle Larga Vendramin, Cannaregio 2040, Tel. +39 041 529 71 11, open daily from 8:15 PM to 3:15 AM, Sundays from 7:00 PM to 2:00 AM, €50 entry fee (includes a €20 gaming chip, one drink, and cloakroom service), ***casinovenezia.it***

7 GIANNI BASSO

The business cards of international stars like Hugh Grant and Angelina Jolie displayed in the shop window serve as the best advertisement for this legendary stampatore. He does not accept credit cards, and his coveted products are not available for online ordering. Before establishing his own business, he worked for many years on Isola San Lazzaro degli Armeni, where he collected his mechanical printing presses.
He insists on personal contact with customers to give each business card an individual touch. Orders take two to five days for delivery. Calle del Fumo, Cannaregio 5306, Tel. +39 041 523 46 81, open Monday to Friday from 9:00 AM to 1:00 PM and from 2:30 PM to 6:00 PM, Saturday from 9:00 AM to 12:00 PM, closed on Sundays.

4 PASTICCERIA DEL MAS

When this small but refined bakery first opened near the train station in 1906, no one could have imagined that decades later, it would find itself wedged between souvenir shops and fast-food stands. Yet, despite the changing surroundings, this beloved pastry shop has held its ground. Early in the morning, locals queue up with their shopping carts to stock up on Pan del Doge and breakfast brioche, while exchanging news at the standing tables. Later in the day, Venice insiders stop by to grab delicious pastries, tramezzini, or biscotti in elegant tin boxes on their way to the train station. Rio Terà Lista di Spagna, Cannaregio 1491, open from 6:30 AM to 7:30 PM, Saturday from 7:00 AM to 7:30 PM, Sunday from 7:30 AM to 7:30 PM.

5 MUSEO EBRAICO DI VENEZIA

For centuries, Jews fleeing persecution found a safe haven in Venice, though their rights were limited. They were allowed to work only as doctors, moneylenders, or second-hand merchants. In the 15th century, several synagogueswere built, but in 1516, a law was enacted that forced all Jews into a ghetto behind locked gates. As a result, the houses on this tiny island were built upward, reaching up to eight stories high. In 1597, the ghetto was dissolved. Today, five historic synagogues and a museum preserve the memory of this period. Campo Ghetto Nuovo, Cannaregio 2902/b, Tel. +39 041 71 53 59, open from 10:00 AM to 5:30 PM, Thursdays until 6:30 PM, closed on Saturdays, ***museoebraico.com***

6 HOTEL TIP PALAZZO ABADASSA

A quiet retreat near the bustling Strada Nova. Maria Luisa Rossi, the owner of this 17th-century palace, welcomes guests to her 15 elegantly decorated rooms and suites, complete with a cozy bar and garden. Calle Priuli, Cannaregio 4011, Tel. +39 041 241 37 84, double rooms from €175, booking via ***tui.com***

DESPAR TEATRO ITALIA 8

This Art Nouveau cinema-theater was inaugurated in 1916, designed by Giovanni Sardi, the same architect responsible for the Excelsior Palace Hotel on the Lido. Its cast iron elements evoke the style of Gustave Eiffel. Once an occasional film set, the building was eventually forgotten – until exactly 100 years later, when an Italian supermarket chaininvested five million euros in its restoration. Today, a gourmet grocery shopping experience in this historic space is truly a feast for the senses. Strada Nova 1939 – 1952, Campiello de l'Anconeta, Cannaregio 1944, ***despar.it***

DORSO DURO

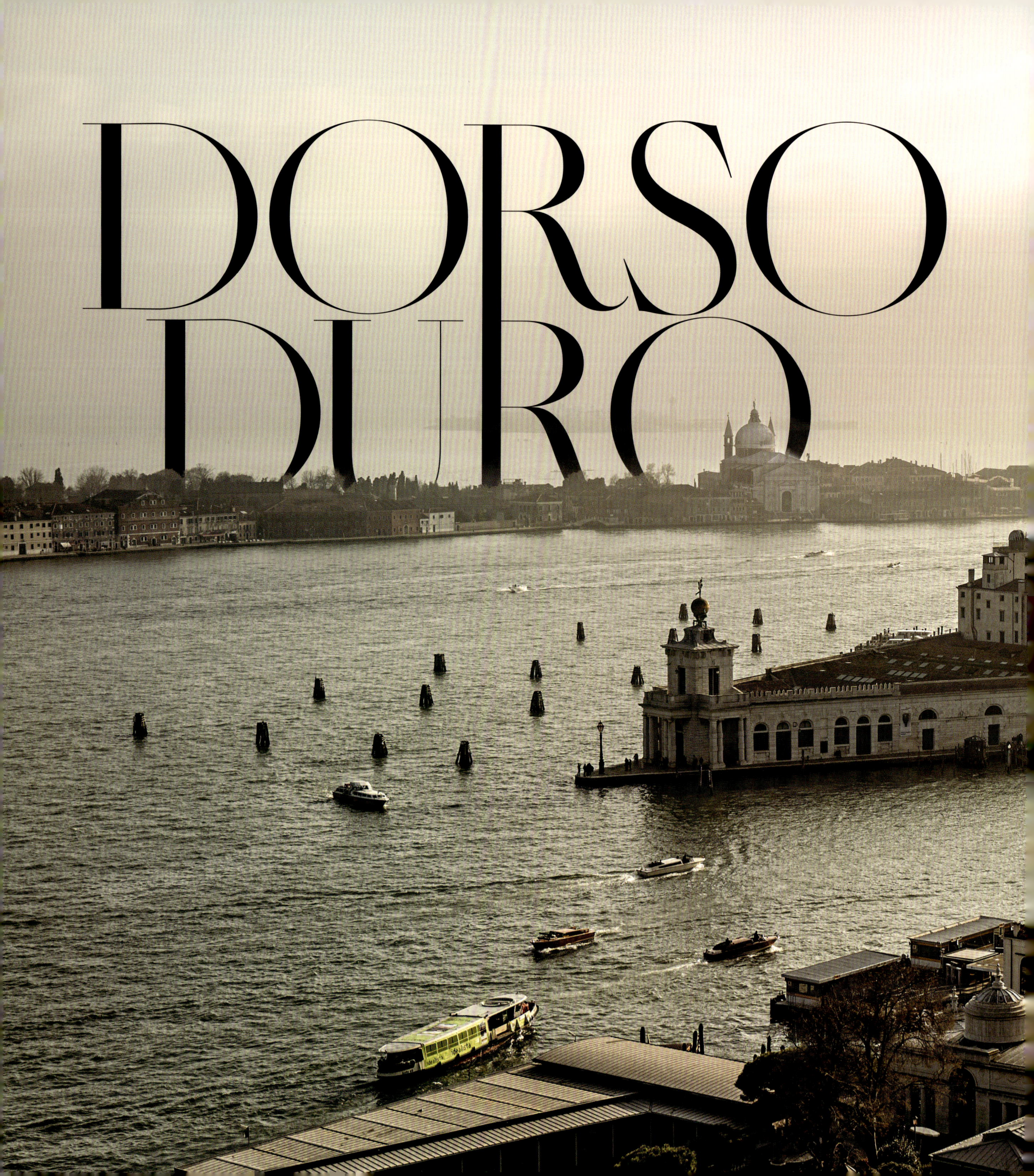

A familiar sight: Venice wrapped in fog.

A rarity in Venice: an active nightlife late into the night.

DORSO DURO

Stylish down to the finest detail the flagship store of Fortuny in Dorsoduro.

Dorsoduro, which borders San Polo and Santa Croce to the south, reveals many different faces. The best way to experience them all is by starting at the Salute Vaporetto stop and walking westward along the entrance to the Grand Canal from the Bacino di San Marco. Here begins a museum district unique to Venice: from the Punta della Dogana, a former customs house now home to contemporary art, to the Pest Church of Santa Maria della Salute, featuring works by Titian and Tintoretto, to the Peggy Guggenheim Collection at Palazzo Venier dei Leoni, the Gallerie dell'Accademia, and the stately Ca' Rezzonico. Turning away from the Grand Canal, you'll pass Rio Squero, one of the last gondola workshops, and follow the path over the Rio degli Alboretti – once a canal, later filled in by the Habsburgs, and today an oleander-lined promenade.

At first glance rather unassuming one of the city's best bookstores.

The city's most popular museum: the Peggy Guggenheim Collection.

One of Venice's landmarks: the Chiesa Madonna della Salute.

This leads to the Zattere, a long waterfront promenade facing the Giudecca Canal, with a view of the island of Giudecca, home to the massive Molino Stucky, now a Hilton hotel. A complete contrast to all this grandeur is Campo Santa Margherita, a lively hub of everyday Venetian life. On the way to Campo Pantalon, keep an eye out just above the waterline – you'll find a graffiti piece by Banksy depicting a small girl in a life vest holding a distress flare.

Caffè Rosso, an insider's spot at Campo Santa Margherita.

One of the many traditional eateries along the canal.

RISTORANTE LINEADOMBRA

A TREASURE TROVE OF FINE WINES

RISTORANTE LINEADOMBRA
PONTE DELL'UMILITÀ
DORSODURO 19
TEL. +39 041-241 18 81
ristorantelineadombra.com

OPENING HOURS:

12:00 PM to 2:15 PM
and 7:00 PM to 9:15 PM
Closed on Tuesdays in winter
and throughout January

Venetian native Marco Bolla fulfilled a long-cherished dream when he took over this hidden gem, tucked away from the tourist crowds. Others had overlooked the restaurant, but he seized the opportunity and has since been both host and proprietor of Lineadombra. Where does the name come from? It was inspired by Joseph Conrad's novella "The Shadow Line," a story about the passage from youth to maturity. The terrace, seemingly floating over the Canale della Giudecca, is fully booked every summer evening. Across the canal lies Giudecca, with the Redentore Church, and to the left, the Isola San Giorgio Maggiore. Inside, the ambiance is equally inviting – the former salt warehouse has been transformed into a striking space where exposed wooden beams contrast with sleek designer chairs, all set to the soft sounds of jazz music. Just a few steps from Punta della Dogana, where ships once docked to unload their cargo, Lineadombra remains deeply connected to Venice's maritime heritage. In the kitchen, Chef Nicola Peressinotto crafts innovative dishes, such as halibut with root vegetables and a carrot-ginger emulsion or scallops in chestnut cream with broccoli and crispy purple potatoes. He is a pioneer of modern Venetian cuisine, steering away from heavy oils, garlic, and rich sauces in favor of a lighter, more refined approach that turns every meal into a delight. A signature touch is his rediscovery of the aromatic herbs and spices that once flooded Venice's markets, at a time when salt alone sufficed in Northern Europe. Since 2004, Lineadombra's wine cellar has been filling with some of the world's finest vintages. Among its treasures: Champagnes from Louis Roederer, Krug, and Ruinart, Amarone and Valpolicella from Veneto, alongside Château Mouton Rothschild, Château Margaux, and Pommard. White wines include Gavi dei Gavi from La Scolca, Chardonnay from Angelo Gaja in Piedmont, and Rieslings from top German estates, as well as Sancerre and Chablis from France.

Left – The restaurant's name pays tribute to a novella by Joseph Conrad.

Below – Lineadombra's terrace – an unbeatable location.

FAVORITE SPOTS

Host Marco Bolla adores Hosteria da Franz for its traditional cuisine and elegant setting (hosteriadafranz.com). Chef Nicola Peressinotto believes Al Sestante deserves a Michelin star and particularly enjoys its rooftop terrace (sestantevenezia.com). Restaurant Manager Andrea Pinton values Osteria Ai Mercanti for its excellent price-performance ratio (aimercanti.it).

TORTELLINI DI RAPA ROSSA ALLA ROBIOLA

RED BEET TORTELLINI WITH ROBIOLA, PUMPKIN SAUCE, AND KING OYSTER MUSHROOMS

SERVES 4
DIFFICULTY

RED BEET TORTELLINI
14.1 oz (400 g) flour
2 eggs
2 egg yolks
3.5 oz (100 g) steamed red beet purée
5.3 oz (150 g) Robiola di Roccaverano
5.3 oz (150 g) ricotta
1 tsp lemon zest

PUMPKIN SAUCE WITH KING OYSTER MUSHROOMS
2 tbsp olive oil
1 garlic clove, minced
10.6 oz (300 g) cardoncelli mushrooms (king oyster mushrooms), diced
10.6 oz (300 g) pumpkin
salt & pepper

TO SERVE
chervil

1 RED BEET TORTELLINI

Combine the flour, eggs, egg yolks, and red beet purée to form a firm, homogeneous dough. Roll it out to 1 mm thickness and cut into twenty 7 x 7 cm squares.
For the filling, blend robiola, ricotta, and lemon zest in a food processor until smooth. Transfer to a piping bag.
Pipe a small amount of filling into the center of each square. Fold into triangles, press the edges together, and connect the two outer corners to shape tortellini. Set aside.

2 PUMPKIN SAUCE WITH KING OYSTER MUSHROOMS

Heat olive oil in a pan. Sauté garlic and mushrooms for a few minutes until golden. Season with salt and pepper.
Boil the pumpkin in salted water until tender, then purée.
Cook the tortellini in salted boiling water for four minutes, drain, and toss gently with the mushrooms.

3 TO SERVE

Divide the pumpkin sauce between plates, arrange the tortellini on top, and finish with the sautéed mushrooms and chervil.

GUANCIA DI VITELLO BRASATA AL PROFUMO DI CAFFÈ

BRAISED VEAL CHEEKS WITH COFFEE AND BROCCOLI-CELERY MILLEFEUILLE

SERVES 4
DIFFICULTY

VEAL CHEEKS
4 veal cheeks
2 tbsp olive oil
3 shallots, chopped
1 celery stalk, chopped
1 carrot, chopped
1 ⅔ cups (400 ml) red wine
½ cup (100 ml) port wine
4 sprigs thyme
1 small handful crushed coffee beans
1 tbsp butter
salt & black peppercorns

BROCCOLI-CELERY MILLEFEUILLE
14.1 oz (400 g) broccoli florets
4 tbsp olive oil
14.1 oz (400 g) celeriac, peeled and sliced into ⅛-inch-thick rounds
salt & pepper

TO SERVE
orange zest

1 **VEAL CHEEKS**
Trim the veal cheeks of excess fat and membrane. In a large pot, heat olive oil and sear the cheeks until golden brown.
Remove and set aside. Sauté shallots, celery, and carrot in the same pot. Return the veal cheeks to the pot, deglaze with red wine and port wine, and add thyme, pepper, and salt. Simmer gently for two hours.
Remove the veal cheeks and keep warm. Strain the cooking liquid, then reduce with the coffee beans until thickened. Strain through a fine cloth and finish with butter.

2 **BROCCOLI-CELERY MILLEFEUILLE**
Blanch the broccoli florets in salted water until tender. Heat olive oil in an ovenproof pan and arrange the celeriac slices inside. Season with salt and pepper and roast at 180°C (350°F) for about one hour. Layer broccoli and celeriac, press down with a weight, then cut into small squares. Reheat in the microwave before serving.

3 **TO SERVE**
Place the veal cheeks on plates, spoon over the coffee-infused sauce, and serve with two millefeuille squares per plate, garnished with orange zest.

TRATTORIA ANZOLO RAFFAELE

FEELING AT HOME WITH FRIENDS

TRATTORIA ANZOLO RAFFAELE
CAMPO DELL'ANGELO RAFFAELE
DORSODURO 1722
TEL. +39 041-523 74 56
trattoriaanzoloraffaele.com

OPENING HOURS:

12:00 - 3:00 PM
7:00 - 10:00 PM
Closed on Wednesdays

Away from the hustle and just a few steps beyond Campo Santa Margherita, Campo Angelo Raffaele is a haven of tranquility. The only restaurant here is as unpretentious and down-to-earth as its menu. Luigi once worked as a tour guide in Venice. When he discovered the 300-year-old, rundown trattoria, he immediately knew what he wanted. From 2003 to 2004, it was carefully renovated. Today, it is mostly Venetians, workers from the Stazione Marittima, and university students who dine here—outdoors in good weather, otherwise inside, surrounded by rustic shelves filled with wine, glassware, beautiful ceramics, and cookbooks that hint at the host's origins. Guests rarely stumble upon this place by chance. "It's important to us that they feel a little at home here," says Luigi. He comes from Sardinia, from the small town of Arbus in the island's southwest. There, he runs a farm, cultivates vineyards, and produces olive oil, saffron, and honey—ingredients he uses in the trattoria and sells in his small shop next door. Since opening the restaurant with his partner Patricia, he has also become a member of the Osti-in-Orto vegetable garden on the lagoon island of Sant'Erasmo. Until 2021, only meat dishes were served here, but that has changed. Venetian-style liver with polenta represents the local cuisine, while ricotta-filled ravioli with orange zest and saffron are a tribute to his Sardinian roots. Luigi and Patricia are also members of the Buona Accoglienza Association Venezia, where restaurant owners and chefs work together to uphold their values—careful selection of ingredients, quality cooking, and professional hospitality. Among the antipasti, a platter of San Daniele prosciutto with wood-fired bread or fresh goat cheese with Tropea red onions is a favorite. A classic pasta dish is Linguine di Gragnano with Piennolo tomato sauce and their own olive oil. Desserts are Patricia's great passion. She loves baking cookies and cakes, creating sweet delights like coffee semifreddo with chocolate sauce or orange-scented crème brûlée. To finish, there are Biscottini to dip into a sweet dessert wine from Friuli.

Left – Patricia, who loves baking cakes and cookies, with manager Paolo.

Below – A hidden oasis of calm: Campo dell'Angelo Raffaele.

FAVORITE SPOTS OF LUIGI UND PATRICIA

We regularly take our small boat into the northern lagoon, weaving through the canals and stopping by our vegetable garden on Sant'Erasmo. Sometimes, we pause at the island of San Francesco del Deserto, home to a community of monks. The best time to visit the monastery is in spring, when nature bursts into bloom and the island is bathed in shades of purple. We also love the Giardini della Biennale – not so much for the exhibitions, but for the positive energy you can feel there.

CASTRAURE DI SANT'ERASMO E BOTTARGA DI MUGGINE DI CABRAS

ARTICHOKES WITH MULLET ROE

SERVES 4
DIFFICULTY

4 Castraure or small artichokes
juice of 1 lemon
1.5 oz (40 g) bottarga (salted, dried mullet roe), thinly sliced
5 tbsp extra virgin olive oil (plus more for serving)
½ tsp salt

1 Trim the stems of the artichokes, remove the tough outer leaves, and snip off the tips of the remaining leaves. Cut them in half lengthwise and place them in a bowl of cold water with the lemon juice.

2 Drain the artichokes and slice them thinly. Season with olive oil and salt. Arrange them alternately with the bottarga slices on four plates. Drizzle with olive oil and serve.

FREGULA CON BEVARASSE

FREGULA WITH BEVARASSE CLAMS

SERVES 4
DIFFICULTY

1 ⅓ lb (600 g) bevarasse or venus clams
2 tbsp extra virgin olive oil
1 garlic clove, crushed
1 bunch parsley, chopped
5 saffron threads
11 oz (320 g) fregula sarda

1 Soak the bevarasse in salted water for 2 hours to remove any sand. Rinse and drain. Heat the olive oil in a medium copper pan with high sides, then lightly sauté the garlic and parsley. Add the bevarasse and saffron, deglaze with 1 ¼ cups of water, and lower the heat. Remove from the heat as soon as the clams open. Discard any closed clams.

2 Cook the pasta in a large pot of salted boiling water according to the package instructions, but drain 3 minutes before it is fully cooked.

3 Reheat the clams, add the fregula, and finish cooking. Divide among four plates and serve hot.

Right – Chef Roberto Gatto returned to Venice after gaining valuable experience around the world.

Below – A postcard-view of the Campanile and Doge's Palace across the Grand Canal.

FAVORITE SPOTS OF ROBERTO GATTO

I love my Sunday walks in the quieter areas of the city, such as Dorsoduro, Sant'Erasmo, and Giudecca. There, I can truly experience absolute freedom and peace. One place especially dear to me is Da Celeste on Pellestrina Island. I love the atmosphere and the traditional Venetian cuisine, particularly the moeche (soft-shell crabs). (daceleste.com)

CIP'S CLUB

CASUAL DINING AT ITS BEST

CIP'S CLUB
BELMOND HOTEL CIPRIANI
GIUDECCA 10
TEL. +39 041-24 08 01
belmond.com

OPENING HOURS:

12:30 PM – 2:30 PM
and 7:30 PM – 10:30 PM

Roberto Gatto is a perfectionist. He experiments with every detail, testing each dish a hundred times until he is satisfied. As a child, he bombarded his mother with endless questions while watching her make pasta and pizza. Later, after soccer practice, he would prepare pasta for his friends. His culinary career began with professional training, followed by 30 years of experience in Switzerland, Los Angeles, Monte Carlo, and Morocco. Now he has returned to Venice as the executive chef at the Belmond Cipriani Hotel on Giudecca Island.

Despite the Cip's Club's dress code – no flip-flops, sleeveless shirts, or shorts for men – the atmosphere remains relaxed. To enjoy a spectacular evening on the terrace overlooking the Canale di Giudecca, with an unobstructed view of the Chiesa della Salute and St. Mark's Square, reservations are essential. Dinner typically starts at 6:30 PM with a Bellini, the Cipriani family's signature cocktail, made from puréed white peaches and Prosecco. Alongside the fine-dining restaurant Oro, Cip's Club is one of the culinary highlights of the Belmond Cipriani. After a temporary closure, Oro has reopened under the leadership of head chef Vania Ghedini from Ferrara, who previously spent five years with the Alajmo group as head chef at Sesamo in Marrakesh's Royal Mansour Hotel. She is advised by Michelin-starred chef Massimo Bottura. As in Harry's Bar, Harry's Dolci (also on Giudecca), and the Locanda Cipriani on Torcello, Cip's Club features Cipriani classics such as carpaccio with its legendary sauce of mayonnaise and Worcestershire sauce and Risotto Primavera made with the finest locally sourced vegetables. The catch of the day is always a good choice, prepared Fritolin-style – pan-fried scampi and calamari served with horseradish mayonnaise and baby zucchini. Meat lovers will appreciate the tender veal chop with cherry tomatoes and arugula. Lunch is light and refreshing. The chef recommends tuna tartare with sun-dried tomatoes, capers, lemon, and basil, often served for sharing. The table settings include exquisite Ginori-Doccia porcelain and hand-blown Murano glassware. Guests not staying in one of the 69 rooms and suites can take advantage of the complimentary 10-minute boat shuttle from St. Mark's Square.

RISOTTO PRIMAVERA

RISOTTO WITH MARKET-FRESH VEGETABLES

SERVES 4
DIFFICULTY

3.5 oz (100 g) butter
½ spring onion, chopped
1.75 oz (50 g) peas
1 oz (30 g) tomatoes, peeled and chopped
1.75 oz (50 g) bell pepper, diced
5.25 oz (150 g) zucchini, diced
1.5 oz (40 g) zucchini blossoms, chopped
1 oz (30 g) carrots, diced
3.5 oz (100 g) green beans, cut into small pieces
3.5 oz (100 g) asparagus
1 artichoke, cooked and chopped
7 oz (200 g) Carnaroli rice
3 cups (750 ml) hot vegetable broth
1.75 oz (50 g) grated Parmigiano Reggiano
salt & pepper

1 Melt 1 ounce of butter in a pan and sauté half the onion. Add the vegetables and briefly sauté. In a separate pot, melt another ounce of butter and soften the remaining onion. Add the rice and toast it while stirring until it turns translucent.

2 Gradually add the hot vegetable broth, letting the rice absorb it little by little while stirring constantly. After 10 minutes, add the sautéed vegetables and continue cooking for another 10 minutes, until all the broth is absorbed and the rice is cooked but not too dry.

3 Remove from heat and allow to cool slightly. Stir in the remaining butter and Parmesan, then season with salt and pepper. Serve immediately.

CIP'S CLUB

CIPPAMISU

A VARIATION OF THE CLASSIC TIRAMISU

SERVES 10
DIFFICULTY

5.3 oz (150 g) egg yolks
5.3 oz (150 g) superfine sugar
17.6 oz (500 g) mascarpone
¼ tsp coffee powder
¾ cup (200 ml) espresso
½ cup (100 ml) Amaretto Disaronno
10 ladyfingers, quartered lengthwise
10 chocolate cups
5 Amaretti cookies, crumbled

TO SERVE
vanilla pudding
chocolate sauce
cocoa powder
10 small chocolate gondolas

1 In a stand mixer, beat the egg yolks and sugar until creamy. Add the mascarpone and coffee powder and mix gently for another 3 minutes, being careful not to overmix, as the mixture should not separate. Transfer the mixture into a piping bag. In a shallow dish, mix the espresso and Amaretto, then dip the quartered ladyfingers into the mixture. Place two quarters into each chocolate cup, pipe a thin layer of mascarpone cream over them, and sprinkle with crumbled Amaretti cookies. Add two more ladyfinger quarters and another layer of mascarpone cream. Refrigerate for at least 6 hours.

2 **TO SERVE**
Spoon some vanilla pudding onto plates, drizzle chocolate sauce over the plates, and use a toothpick to create decorative swirls. Dust the tiramisu with cocoa powder, place a chocolate gondola on top, and set the chocolate cups in the sauce. Serve immediately.

CIP'S
CLUB

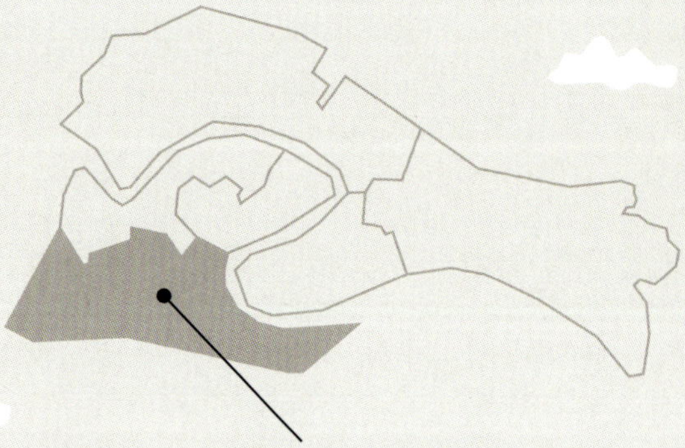

DORSO-DURO

1 HOTEL TIP: PENSIONE ACCADEMIA

A pioneer among Venice's boutique hotels, this charming 17th-century villa, Villa Maravege, opened its doors to paying guests in the late 1940s under the Salmaso family. Its 27 beautifully decorated rooms are frequently booked out. What guests appreciate most: the prime location on the Grand Canal and the lush gardens on either side, where they can enjoy breakfast, read in a swing seat, and forget about time. Fondamenta Bollani, Dorsoduro 1058, Tel. +39 041 521 01 88, double rooms from €270, ***pensioneaccademia.it***

2 ISOLA DELLA GIUDECCA

The Swiss-German industrialist Giovanni Stucky gave his name to Italy's largest grain mill before the fascists seized it, leaving the imposing red-brick building abandoned for decades. In 2007, it was reborn as the Hilton Molino Stucky, home to Venice's highest rooftop terrace – perfect for a sundowner (hilton.com). Other highlights include the Spazio Punch arts and cultural center (spaziopunch.com) and Trattoria La Palanca, a local favorite for lunch (Calle Giazzo, Dorsoduro 448). During the annual Festa del Redentore, the Redentore Church, built in 1577 to thank God for delivering Venice from the plague, becomes a major pilgrimage site.

3 GALLERIE DELL' ACCADEMIA

This building has had many lives: first as a church, then a monastery, later the Scuola della Carità, before Carlo Scarpa transformed it in the 1940s into one of Venice's most important art museums. It houses an extraordinary collection of Venetian masterpieces, including Carpaccio's works, a vast cycle of paintings by Tintoretto, Titian's Pietà – his final painting before dying of the plague in 1576 – and the only Canaletto piece in his hometown, which secured his admission into the Academy.
Recently expanded, the museum also serves as an exhibition space during the Biennale. Campo della Carità, Dorsoduro 1050, Tel. +39 041 522 22 47, open from 8:15 AM to 7:15 PM, Mondays until 2:00 PM, ***gallerie-accademia.it***

4 OSTERIA ENOTECA AI ARTISTI

Chef Francesca Ciancio creates a daily menu based on what catches her eye at the Rialto Market – much to the delight of both owner Vincenzo Buonfiglio and a loyal following of regular guests. She keeps things simple but uses the best ingredients, serving dishes like maltagliati pasta with shrimp, garlic, chili, and artichokes or pork ribs with seasonal vegetables. Excellent house wines complement the menu. Fondamenta della Toletta, Dorsoduro 1169/a, Tel. +39 041 523 89 44, open from 12:45 to 2:45 PM and 7:00 to 10:00 PM, closed Sundays and Mondays.

5 CAMPO SANTA MARGHERITA

At the western end of Dorsoduro lies Venice's second-largest and arguably second-most beautiful square, after St. Mark's. It lacks grandiose architecture but exudes an authentic, everyday charm that is increasingly rare in the city. Housewives with shopping trolleys chat on sunlit benches, best friends sip wine at Al Bocon Di Vino, enjoying meatballs and an ombra(a small glass of wine).
The square is home to excellent coffee, cocktails, and spritz served with small bites, available until 1:00 AM. Dorsoduro 2963, Tel. +39 041 528 79 98

6 GELATERIA NICO

Few things are as enjoyable as ending a summer stroll along the Zattere waterfront with a stop here, in a prime location with a view of Giudecca Island. Since 1937, the terrace of Gelateria Nico has been a pilgrimage site for ice cream lovers, including celebrities like Peggy Guggenheim and Angelina Jolie.
Beyond a vast selection of classic flavors, they serve their legendary semifreddo specialty: Gianduiotto, a dreamy mix of chocolate, nougat, hazelnuts, and whipped cream. Fondamenta Zattere al Ponte Lungo, Dorsoduro 922, Tel. +39 041 522 52 93, open Friday to Wednesday from 6:30 AM to 9:00 PM, closed Thursdays and in January, ***gelaterianico.com***

COLLEZIONE PEGGY GUGGENHEIM

7

Almost every palazzo on the Grand Canal could tell a thousand stories. Palazzo Barbaro once housed the writer Henry James, Palazzo Mocenigo was home to the eccentric poet Lord Byron, and the politically controversial Italian writer Gabriele d'Annunzio is said to have plotted a revolution in the Casa Rossa. Directly across the canal stands the distinctive low-profile Palazzo Venier dei Leoni. After the extravagant fashion icon Luisa Casati, known for her legendary parties, the American heiress Peggy Guggenheim moved in in 1949, where she remained for the rest of her life. She is buried in the garden alongside her 14 Lhasa Apso dogs, as per her wishes. As one of the most passionate collectors of modern art in her time, she left behind nearly 200 paintings and sculptures by artists such as Picasso, Dalí, Magritte, Duchamp, Braque, Pollock, Kandinsky, de Chirico, and Max Ernst – the latter of whom she was married to for two years. She had adresses, and traveled through Venice in her private gondola. When she passed away in 1979, the city lost one of its most flamboyant personalities.
Dorsoduro 701 – 704, Tel. +39 041 240 54 11, open from 10:00 AM to 6:00 PM, closed on Tuesdays, ***guggenheim-venice.it***

LAGOON

280

A quick break from the kitchen: fresh air and a moment of rest.

Aerial approach over the lagoon on the way to Venice's airport.

LAGOON

Shaped by the rhythm of the tides and the interplay of the sea with the tributary rivers that flow into it, the Venetian Lagoon is a vast shallow body of water interwoven with salt marshes, sandbanks, and numerous tiny islets. Of the 120 larger islands, only about a dozen are inhabited. Visitors who venture beyond the usual tourist hotspots will find time well spent exploring these lagoon islands. Three of the northern lagoon's most famous islands stand out: Torcello, where it all began – the first settlers found refuge here as early as the 7th century. Murano, forever synonymous with its centuries-old glassmaking tradition, which dazzles travelers in the form of grand chandeliers hanging from the ceilings of five-star hotels around the world. Burano, with its vibrant houses, fishing boats, intricate lacework, and its smaller sister island Mazzorbo, home to lush gardens and vineyards. Completely dedicated to vegetable farming, Sant'Erasmo, the lagoon's largest island, and Vignole, with its prized violet artichokes, supply Venice's

Venetians remain pedestrians for life.

A view from Venissa's vineyards towards Mazzorbo's bell tower.

Unmistakable: the candy-colored fishermen's house of Burano.

Perfect for a stroll: the canal-side promenades of Burano.

Mazzorbo: Fresh herbs from the gardens of Venissa.

top chefs with fresh produce. To the south, two long, narrow islands separate Venice from the Adriatic: Lido, famous for its sandy beaches and the annual film festival, and Pellestrina, its quieter, less populated neighbor, marked by imposing ten-meter-high marble and stone seawalls. The lesser-known small islands have played various roles throughout history – as quarantine stations, leper colonies, mental asylums, plague hospitals, and monastic retreats, or simply as outposts for fishermen and duck hunters. In recent years, some of these islands have transformed into exclusive luxury retreats and island resorts – a serene alternative to the bustling city streets of Venice.

A reason to stay: modern vacation apartments in Burano's historic homes.

RISTORANTE ADRIATICO TERRACE

GRANDHOTEL-GRANDEZZA

RISTORANTE ADRIATICO TERRACE, LIDO
AT EXCELSIOR VENICE LIDO RESORT
LUNGOMARE GUGLIELMO MARCONI 41
LIDO DI VENEZIA
TEL. +39 041-526 02 01
hotelexcelsiorvenezia.com

OPENING HOURS:

Daily from 7:30 PM to 10:30 PM

Where the poet and naturalist Johann Wolfgang Goethe collected sea snails and shore crabs on the beach during his journey to Italy in 1786, only about 300 people lived a hundred years later. At that time, the Lido, this twelve-kilometer-long narrow strip of land between the lagoon and the Adriatic, along with the small neighboring island of Pellestrina, was still seen as a kind of protective barrier against natural forces. It was only when the glamorous Grand Hotel Des Bains opened in July 1900, attracting an illustrious crowd to the Lido, that things began to change. Especially when Thomas Mann was inspired during his stay in 1911 to write the novella Death in Venice, which gained even greater fame in 1971 with Visconti's film adaptation, the hotel became a legend. Today, it stands boarded up, though since 2023, the Des Bains 1900 Luxury Beach Club has been in operation. In contrast, the magnificent Excelsior Venice Lido Resort, which opened in 1908, remains a steadfast beacon. The private cabanas on the beach are highly coveted, as are the newly designed suites on the fifth floor and the fifteen suites traditionally decorated in classic Moorish style. At the Excelsior, the beach season traditionally begins at the end of May, and since 1932, the Excelsior Palace has hosted the film festival each September, marking the close of the bathing season. Guests begin an unforgettable evening by sipping a cocktail or a glass of Prosecco with cicchetti at sunset in one of the many nostalgic beach cabanas. Chef Alessandro Ramella, a protégé of Gualtiero Marchesi, crafts the finest flavors of the lagoon and the Adriatic in the gourmet restaurant Adriatico Terrace. Originally from the small Lombard town of Mortara, he spent his childhood Sundays in the kitchen with his mother, absorbing fundamental culinary knowledge. Whenever he visits her, he reflects on the simple culinary principles that have guided him throughout his career. His journey has taken him through various Michelin-starred and fine-dining establishments in Italy, but he undoubtedly honed his skills at the two-star restaurant in Brescia under the tutelage of Gualtiero Marchesi. Alessandro Ramella is supported by award-winning sommelier Lino Marchese, known for his light and refreshing cocktails like Cool as Cucumber, a summer drink with melon, pineapple, and fresh cucumber. Ramella also oversees the Elimar Beach Bar & Restaurant, the Blue Bar, and the Pool Bar. In summer, guests can also enjoy the delicious specialties of L'Antica Pizzeria da Michele, which gained worldwide fame through the film Eat, Pray, Lovestarring Julia Roberts. Alongside Neapolitan classics like Margherita and Marinara, the Excelsior features signature pizzas created exclusively for the resort. Since 2024, the Excelsior has also partnered with the champagne house Compte de Montaigne, whose sparkling selections are served in all bars and through room service. From spring to autumn, as long as the Excelsior is open, a private yacht shuttle takes guests to St. Mark's Square in just under fifteen minutes.

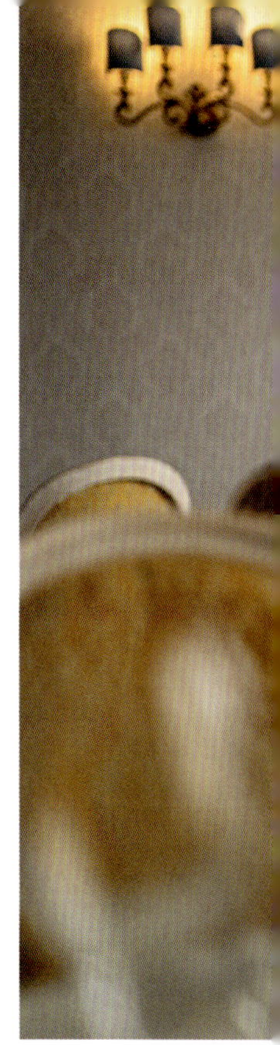

Left – The photographs on the walls of the Adriatico Terrace recall visits from famous guests.

Below – Hosting the Venice Film Festival since 1932: the Excelsior.

FAVORITE SPOTS OF ALESSANDRO RAMELLA

My personal chill-out spots are the island of Giudecca and the small fishing village of Malamocco on the Lido. Giudecca has this cool, calming vibe and absolutely unbeatable views of Venice and the sea. And then there's Malamocco. It's quite a journey to get there, but it's worth it. I prefer to bike the route. Malamocco feels as though time has stood still. The charm of this little fishing village, combined with a light sea breeze – pure magic.

RE & REGINA

KING & QUEEN RISOTTO

SERVES 1

DIFFUCULTY

SEASONED BUTTER

1.75 oz (50 g) finely chopped white onions
2 tbsp (30 ml) white wine
2 tbsp (30 ml) white wine vinegar
0.7 oz (20 g) sour cream butter

RISOTTO

1 tbsp butter
2.5 oz (70 g) Carnaroli San Massimo Riserva rice
4 tbsp (50 ml) white wine
1 ¼ cups (300 ml) light chicken broth
0.2 oz (5 g) katsuobushi (bonito flakes)
0.5 oz (15 g) Parmigiano Reggiano
seasoned butter (see above)
2 tsp (10 ml) Blanc de Blancs Champagne
0.07 oz (2 g) organic lemon zest
chopped chives
salt

TO SERVE

0.35 oz (10 g) Da Vinci Ars Italica caviar
0.03 oz (1 g) gold leaf

1 **SEASONED BUTTER**

Place the onions with the white wine and white wine vinegar in a small saucepan and cook until translucent and the liquid has almost entirely evaporated. Add the butter in small pieces, stirring until melted. Strain through a sieve into a sealable container and allow to set in the refrigerator.

2 **RISOTTO**

Melt the butter in a saucepan and toast the rice. Season with salt and deglaze with white wine. Bring the chicken broth to a boil and pour it over the bonito flakes.
Once the wine has fully evaporated, gradually add the hot broth while stirring constantly. Cook the risotto for about 16 minutes until the rice is tender but still al dente. Remove from heat and stir in the Parmesan, seasoned butter, and champagne. Finish with lemon zest and chives.

3 **TO SERVE**

Spoon the risotto onto a black, flat plate and garnish with caviar and gold leaf.

BRANZINO CON SALSA DI OSTRICHE

SEA BASS WITH OYSTER SAUCE

SERVES 4
DIFFICULTY

7 oz (200 g) white asparagus
7 oz (200 g) green asparagus
12 fresh oysters
½ cup (100 ml) fish broth
4.2 oz (120 g) butter
0.1 oz (3 g) Colatura di Alici di Cetara (fish sauce)
1 pinch xanthan
3 tbsp olive oil
4 sea bass fillets
1 caper leaf, finely sliced
salt & pepper

1 Place the white and green asparagus in a vacuum-sealed bag with 4 cups of water and 1.75 oz salt. Seal the bag and cook sous vide in steam at 185°F for about 20 minutes until tender but still crisp. Remove, drain, and set aside.

2 For the oyster sauce, steam the oysters for 2 minutes at 212°F, reserving the liquid they release. Remove the oysters from their shells and blend them with 1.7 fl oz of the cooking liquid, fish broth, butter, and Colatura di Alici. Add a pinch of xanthan and blend until smooth and velvety.

3 Heat the olive oil to 410°F. Place the sea bass fillets skin-side up on a sieve and pour the hot oil over them to crisp the skin. Then, cook the fillets without additional fat, searing the flesh side until just cooked through.

4 Arrange the asparagus on four plates, place the sea bass fillets skin-side up on top, and spoon the oyster sauce around them. Garnish with caper leaf strips, salt, and plenty of pepper before serving.

TRATTORIA AL GATTO NERO

THE VIOLET HOUSE

TRATTORIA AL GATTO NERO
FONDAMENTA DELLA
GIUDECCA 88
TEL. +39041-73 01 20
gattonero.com

OPENING HOURS:

12:30 PM – 3:00 PM
and 7:30 PM – 10:30 PM
Closed Sunday evening,
Monday, Wednesday evening,
and Thursday evening

Given that most visitors to Venice are day-trippers, the lagoon remains a quiet and safe retreat. Only those who stay longer eventually venture out to the islands of the lagoon, gaining an insight into what daily life in and around Venice truly entails. They begin to understand the impact of the tides on this delicate aquatic landscape, the role of islands like Lido and Pellestrina in protecting the Serenissima, the cemetery island of San Michele where Venetians lay their dead to rest, and, last but not least, islands like Sant'Erasmo, Giudecca, and Vignole, which serve as vegetable gardens for the city. As in Venice itself, the population on the islands has declined. Altogether, fewer than 3,000 people live there. The island of Burano, with its dollhouse-like, candy-colored fishermen's houses along the canals, is so charming that French star architect Philippe Starck is said to own three properties here. The most famous resident was composer Baldassare Galuppi, born on Burano in 1706. The central piazza and main street bear his name. A useful landmark for island explorers is the leaning bell tower of Chiesa San Martino, which houses a remarkable Crucifixion scene by Giovanni Battista Tiepolo. Anyone who has visited Burano will remember the bright violet house on Fondamenta Giudecca, with a few Thonet chairs and tables set outside in the sun for guests. In 1965, Ruggero Bovo and his wife Lucia took over an old osteria here and quickly transformed it into a thriving seafood restaurant. Today, under the leadership of their son Massimiliano, fish and seafood still take center stage on the menu. The focus is on simple, honest preparation. The selection is extensive, with most ingredients sourced from the lagoon – razor clams (cannolicchi), crabs sautéed in olive oil, tiny shrimp served on a bed of soft polenta, scallops (capesante), mussels, and mantis shrimp. Among the pasta dishes, tagliolini with spider crab is a particular favorite. The catch of the day is either grilled or pan-fried. From the Vaporetto station at Fondamenta Nove, Burano can be reached in about 45 minutes via Line 12.

Left – Fisherman and host since 1965: Ruggero Bovo.

Below – A guest favorite: the charming outdoor seating.

FAVORITE SPOTS OF RUGGERO BOVO

There is a special place I always return to – the Scuola Grande di San Rocco. Since the 15th century, it has been the prestigious seat of a brotherhood. What fascinates me every time is the cycle of 57 paintings by Tintoretto (scuolagrandesanrocco.org).

SPAGHETTI CON FORBICI DI GRANCHIO E FIORI DI ZUCCHINA

SPAGHETTI WITH CRAB CLAWS AND ZUCCHINI BLOSSOMS

SERVES 2
DIFFICULTY

14 oz (400 g) spaghetti
14 oz (400 g) crab claws, fresh or frozen
12 zucchini blossoms
1 onion, finely chopped
2 garlic cloves, finely chopped
1 red chili, finely chopped (optional)
½ cup (125 ml) white wine
¼ cup (60 ml) chopped fresh parsley
4 tbsp olive oil
salt & pepper to taste

1 Cook the spaghetti according to the package instructions in salted water.
While the pasta cooks, sear the crab claws in a large pan with 2 tbsp olive oil over medium heat until fully cooked and pink. Remove from the pan and set aside.
In the same pan, sauté the onion, garlic, and chili (if using) over medium heat until soft. Add the white wine and bring to a simmer. Reduce the heat and let simmer for 5 minutes until the liquid has reduced by half. Add the zucchini blossoms and cook for another 2 minutes until tender.
Return the crab claws to the pan, add the parsley, salt, and pepper, and mix well.
Drain the spaghetti and toss it with the sauce in the pan. Serve immediately.

BIGOLI CON GAMBERI, CARCIOFI FRESCHI E POMODORI CILIEGINI

BIGOLI WITH SHRIMP, FRESH ARTICHOKES, AND CHERRY TOMATOES

SERVES 4
DIFFICULTY

12 oz (350 g) bigoli pasta
14 oz (400 g) shrimp, peeled and deveined
4 fresh artichokes
7 oz (200 g) cherry tomatoes
2 garlic cloves, finely chopped
½ onion, finely chopped
2 tbsp olive oil
½ cup (125 ml) white wine
½ cup (125 ml) chicken broth
½ cup (125 ml) heavy cream
salt & pepper to taste
fresh basil for garnish (optional)

1 Clean the artichokes by trimming off the stem and removing the tough lower leaves. Cut off the outer leaves down to the pale green part. Trim the tip of the artichoke and use scissors to snip off about a third of the remaining leaves. Drizzle the artichokes with lemon juice to prevent browning. Bring a large pot of water to a boil, adding some salt and the juice of one lemon. Place the artichokes upside down in the boiling water and simmer for about 20 – 25 minutes until tender. Remove from the water and let cool slightly. Once cool enough to handle, remove the stem and scrape out the choke with a knife. Cut the hearts into bite-sized pieces.

2 Cook the bigoli according to the package instructions in salted water. Pat the shrimp dry with paper towels and season with salt and pepper. Halve the cherry tomatoes.

3 Heat the olive oil in a large pan and sauté the shrimp over medium heat for about 2 minutes per side until pink and cooked through. Remove the shrimp from the pan and set aside. In the same pan, sauté the onion and garlic over medium heat for about 3 minutes until soft. Add the white wine and bring to a boil, then reduce the heat and let it simmer for 2 minutes until the liquid reduces. Add the chicken broth and heavy cream, bring to a boil, then add the artichoke pieces and cherry tomatoes. Simmer for about 5 minutes until the artichokes are tender.

4 Return the shrimp and cooked bigoli to the pan and toss to combine. Season with salt and pepper. Serve garnished with fresh basil.

RISTORANTE VENISSA

A WINERY WITH MICHELIN-STARRED CUISINE

VENISSA
FONDAMENTA SANTA CATERINA 3
ISOLA DI MAZZORBO
TEL. +39 041-527 22 81
venissa.it/casaburano.it

OPENING HOURS:

12:30 PM – 2:00 PM
and 7:30 PM – 9:00 PM
Closed on Wednesdays in September
Closed on Tuesdays and Wednesdays in all other months

Until a few years ago, few people knew where to find the island of Mazzorbo. For most, it was simply the last Vaporetto stop before Burano – let alone a place they'd associate with Winston Churchill, who once painted here with great enthusiasm during his visit to Venice. That all changed abruptly when Gianluca Bisol, a renowned Prosecco producer from Valdobbiadene, arrived to purchase an abandoned vineyard. The ancient stone walls surrounding it, dating back to the 13th century, were originally built to protect the vines from flooding. As Venice expanded and began importing wine from outside the city, the vineyard on Mazzorbo lost its viability. Bisol and his team discovered a few surviving vines of Dorona, a grape used in the Renaissance to produce a golden-hued white wine, thought to have been extinct since the catastrophic flood of 1966. Today, there are 4,000 Dorona vines once again, forming the heart of Scarpa Volo, the small vineyard that Bisol revived. In 2012, he was able to harvest for the first time, and since then, the harvest takes place every September. The grapes are transported in refrigerated trucks to Montalcino, where winemaker Roberto Cipreso oversees their fermentation. The wine is then stored in glass containers and transferred to Valdobbiadene for bottling – about 3,000 bottles per year. Today, Venissa Bianco appears on the wine lists of Venice's finest restaurants. Connoisseurs appreciate its delicate notes of apricot and apple, along with a faint saline touch. In a nod to Venice's historical battiloro (goldbeaters), the wine's labels are adorned with an ultra-thin layer of gold leaf. The estate's former farmhouse has been transformed into a romantic guesthouse with five rooms, while the pavilion at the vineyard's edge now attracts gourmets to its restaurant, Venissa. On pleasant days, life unfolds on the terrace and in the garden. The kitchen is helmed by Chiara Pavan and Francesco Brutto, whose philosophy, Cucina Ambientale, underscores their commitment to protecting the fragile lagoon environment. In 2021, Venissa received a Green Michelin Star. Guests choose between two tasting menus – one with seven courses and one with ten. Naturally, there is an on-site kitchen garden, and even the historic fish pond has been reactivated. The estate's second restaurant, Osteria Contemporanea, specializes in traditional Venetian cuisine. Guests can share cicchetti, pasta, risotto, fish, and vegetarian dishes in a relaxed, communal dining style. The adjacent bar is open daily, offering a perfect setting for a glass of wine, a cocktail, and delicious small plates. In addition to Venissa Bianco, the winery now produces Rosso Venissa, a full-bodied red wine made from Merlot and Carménère grapes grown in a historic vineyard on the nearby island of Santa Cristina. Guests who wish to stay overnight can choose between accommodations at the vineyard or at Casa Burano, which offers 13 rooms spread across five restored fishermen's houses on Burano. Furnished with modern Italian design pieces, guests enjoy breakfast together at Venissa, just a ten-minute walk away – Burano and its smaller sister island, Mazzorbo, are connected by a bridge.

Far left – Guests enjoy drinks and small bites at the bar all day long.

Left – A power couple: Francesco Brutto and Chiara Pavan.

Below – Casual dining with a view of lush greenery at Osteria Contemporanea.

FAVORITE SPOTS OF CHIARA AND FRANCESCO

From the Vaporetto stop Ca' D'Oro, it's just a short walk to Trattoria Vini da Gigio. Siblings Laura and Paolo Lazzari are known for their carefully curated wine selection. We like to start our meal with a plate of raw ham and grilled artichokes or a spider crab salad, followed by seared beef strips with arugula, Parmesan, and balsamic. A Friulian blend or a Blanc de Morgex from the Aosta Valley pairs perfectly (vinidagigio.com). Another favorite spot, also in the Cannaregio district, is Osteria Giorgione da Masa, where we enjoy a Japanese twist on Venetian cicchetti (osteriagiorgionedamasa.com).

RAVIOLI RIPIENI CON ZUPPA DI PESCE

FILLED RAVIOLI WITH FISH SOUP, GINGER OIL, AND SEAWEED SALAD

SERVES 4
DIFFICULTY

GINGER OIL
1 ¾ oz (50 g) chopped ginger
½ cup (100 ml) extra virgin olive oil

PASTA DOUGH
15 oz (420 g) 00 flour
2 ½ oz (70 g) extra fine breadcrumbs
4 eggs
2 egg yolks
1 tbsp extra virgin olive oil
1 pinch salt

FILLING
7 oz (200 g) mullet
7 oz (200 g) monkfish
10 ½ oz (300 g) blue crab
7 oz (200 g) double-concentrated tomato paste
2 tbsp extra virgin olive oil
1 garlic clove, chopped
3 gelatin sheets
¾ cup (200 ml) white wine
1 clove
2 sprigs parsley

SEAWEED SALAD
1.1 lbs (500 g) mussels, cleaned
4 Swiss chard leaves
4 kale leaves
4 curly lettuce leaves, coarsely chopped
4 red radicchio leaves, coarsely chopped
2 tbsp lemon juice

1 **GINGER OIL**
The night before, mix the chopped ginger with the olive oil and let it infuse overnight. Strain the next day.

2 **PASTA DOUGH**
Place 3 ½ oz of flour and the breadcrumbs in a baking dish and roast in the oven at 375°F until lightly browned. Knead the remaining flour with the eggs, egg yolks, olive oil, and salt until smooth. Shape into a ball, cover, and let rest.

3 **FILLING**
Fillet and debone the fish, setting the flesh aside. Roast the fish bones in the oven. Once browned, add the remaining bones and cover with water and 2 tbsp tomato paste. Let simmer. Finely chop ¾ of the fish meat and the crab meat. Heat olive oil in a pan, sauté the garlic, then add the remaining fish, the clove, and parsley. Mix with 3 ½ fl oz white wine and heat.

Soak the gelatin sheets in cold water. Meanwhile, strain the fish stock through a fine sieve, add the gelatin, and refrigerate until fully set. Once firm, whip the gelatin-fish stock mixture and combine with the sautéed fish. Purée and transfer to a piping bag.

4 **RAVIOLI**
Roll out the pasta dough thinly and cut into squares. Pipe the filling onto the center of one square, place another square on top, and press the edges together. Keep chilled until ready to use.

5 **SEAWEED SALAD**
Place the mussels with a little water in a pot and steam covered until they open. Discard any unopened mussels and remove the shells. Reserve the mussel liquid and let cool. Fully submerge the mussels in the cooled liquid and set aside. Reserve the remaining liquid.
Remove the central ribs and veins from the chard and kale leaves. Bring the reserved mussel liquid to a boil with the lemon juice and pour over half the salad leaves. Set the remaining leaves aside.

6 **TO SERVE**
Season the reserved salad leaves with ginger oil and salt. Cook the ravioli in boiling water and drain once they rise to the surface. Heat olive oil in a pan, lightly sauté the ravioli, then plate in soup bowls. Garnish with seaweed salad, steamed mussels, and the dressed salad leaves.

CREPE ALLE ERBE CON GELATO AL ROSMARINO

HERB CRÊPES WITH ROSEMARY ICE CREAM

SERVES 4
DIFFICULTY

ROSEMARY ICE CREAM
3 ¼ cups (800 ml) whole milk
¾ cup (200 g) heavy cream
7 oz (200 g) fresh rosemary
7 oz (200 g) egg yolks
7 oz (200 g) sugar

HERB CREAM
1.4 oz (40 g) lovage
1.75 oz (50 g) tarragon
2 ½ (600 ml) cups milk
3 eggs
2.8 oz (80 g) melted butter
5 oz (140 g) flour
0.07 oz (2 g) salt

BATTER
2 oz (60 g) fresh basil
2 cups (500 ml) whole milk
3.5 oz (100 g) egg yolks
1.6 oz (45 g) cornstarch
4.2 oz (120 g) sugar

TO SERVE
7 oz (200 g) butter
1 tbsp sugar Absinthe Leaves from: basil, mint, tarragon, sage, thyme, absinthe, oregano, fennel, nasturtium, marjoram, sorrel, etc.

1 **ROSEMARY ICE CREAM**
Heat the milk and cream in a saucepan, stirring constantly until it reaches a boil. Remove from heat, add the fresh rosemary, and let steep overnight. The next day, strain out the rosemary and reheat the milk-cream mixture. Add the egg yolks and sugar, stirring constantly, until the mixture thickens at 180°F. Let cool, then churn in a Pacojet or ice cream maker.

2 **HERB CREAM**
Blend the lovage and tarragon with 7 fl oz of milk, then strain through a clean cloth. Add the remaining ingredients and mix well. Chill the mixture in the refrigerator for 4-5 hours.

3 **BATTER**
Blend the basil with the milk and strain through a clean cloth. Whisk the egg yolks, cornstarch, and sugar together. Heat the milk while stirring constantly, then gradually add a few tablespoons of hot milk to the egg mixture, stirring well. Carefully combine the egg mixture with the remaining hot milk, return to the heat, and whisk until thickened.

4 **TO SERVE**
Cook thin crêpes in a non-stick pan. Let them cool, then fill with the herb cream. Roll up the crêpes and sauté them in butter and sugar, then drizzle with absinthe. Garnish with a selection of fresh herb leaves and serve with rosemary ice cream.

LAGOON

SANTA CRISTINA

1

This private little island in the northern lagoon owes its success story to a rescue operation. Nearly a decade ago, René Deutsch, the stepson of Gernot Langes-Swarovski, and his wife Sandra began transforming the island into a sanctuary of meditative tranquility. The groundwork had already been laid by Swarovski, who initiated the drying of marshlands, the revival of fish ponds, and the construction of a family retreat, all in accordance with sustainable principles. Today, the fish farm thrives, powered by the natural ebb and flow of the tides. Sea bass, sea bream, mussels, and crabs supply the top restaurants of the lagoon. The island also produces olive oil and honey, while, with the expertise of the Venissa winery on Mazzorbo, its vineyard has been brought back to life.
For ten weeks each year, Villa Ammiana is available as an exclusive vacation rental for a maximum of 16 guests, complete with a private chef and service staff, ***veniceprivateisland.com.***

2 ORTO DI VENEZIA, SANT'ERASMO

The second-largest island in the lagoon is protected from flooding and lies between Burano and Murano. For Michel Thoulouze, a successful French film and television producer, acquiring a vineyard on Sant'Erasmo was a lifelong dream. But before he could plant a single vine, eleven hectares of land had to be cleared of wild blackberry thickets.
With wine experts from the Rhône Valley by his side, he selected Vermentino, Malvasia Istriana, and Fiano as the vineyard's grape varieties. In 2008, the newcomer released his first vintage, and today, his wines are served by Michelin-starred chefs, including Alain Ducasse in Paris. Tours and tastings by appointment. Via de le Motte 1, Tel. +39 348 872 75 00 Open Tuesday to Thursday, 10:00 AM - 12:30 PM and 2:30 PM - 6:00 PM, ***ortodivenezia.com***

3 AEOROPORTO GIOVANNI NICELLI, LIDO

When the lagoon's only small airport opened in 1935, air traffic was still booming. Until 1953, Nicelli was Venice's official airport. Today, it occasionally welcomes private jets, but it has reinvented itself as a cultural center. Following its first exhibition during the 2022 Biennale, the airport now hosts events, workshops, and film screenings. Since its renovation in 2019, Fly Restaurant has become a great spot for lunch and dinner.
Via Morandi 9, Tel. +39 041 312 39 84 Open Tuesday to Sunday, 12:30 PM – 2:00 PM and 7:00 PM – 9:30 PM, closed Mondays ***aeroportonicelli.com***

4 MUSEO DEL MERLETTO, BURANO

Burano has been famous beyond Italy's borders for its exquisite lacework for over 500 years. In the past, its ultra-delicate bridal veils, created using a unique air-stitching method, traveled as far as the court of Louis XIV in Paris. Today, only a few artisans on the island still master this rare craft. The history of Burano's lace is beautifully preserved in the Museo del Merletto, located in the former lace school in the Palazzo del Podestà. Visitors can explore the intricate art of lace through a fascinating film and a collection of historical pieces. Piazza Baldassare Galuppi 187, Tel. +39 041 73 00 34 Open from mid-May to late September, Tuesday to Sunday, 10:00 AM – 4:00 PM ***museomerletto.it***.
Shopping tip: For high-quality lacework, visit Dalla Lidia Merletti d'Arte.
Via Baldassare Galuppi 215, Tel. +39 041 73 00 52 ***dallalidia.com***

5 BASILICA DI SANTA MARIA ASSUNTA, TORCELLO

Dedicated in the 7th century, this remarkable church exemplifies Venetian-Byzantine architecture and has undergone multiple restorations. Its breathtaking mosaics, multicolored marble floors, and magnificent dome make it a must-visit for those venturing to the northernmost reaches of the lagoon. Not to be missed: Museo Provinciale di Torcello, housed in two simple palaces. Archaeological treasures, including ceramics, busts, and amphorae, reveal the early history of Venice. Open daily: May – October, 10:30 AM – 5:30 PM; November – April, 10:00 AM – 5:00 PM. Island walks often conclude at the Osteria al Ponte del Diavolo, a charming terrace restaurant near the legendary Devil's Bridge. Tel. +39 041 73 04 01, ***osteriaalpontedeldiavolo.com***

MURANO GLASS ART 6

The museum dedicated to the history of glass art since 1861, housed in Palazzo Giustinian, welcomes visitors with around 4,000 exhibits spanning from antiquity to the modern era. Fondamenta Giustinian 8, Tel. +39 041 73 95 86, open from April to October from 10:00 AM to 6:00 PM and from November to February from 10:00 AM to 5:00 PM, ***museovetro.visitmuve.it***
The restaurant Vetri at Punta Conterie, a modern cultural center dedicated to glass art in a former glass factory, is an excellent lunch spot. Fondamenta Giustinian 1, Tel. +39 041 527 51 74, ***puntaconterie.com***
Palazzo Barovier & Toso With 700 years of history, Barovier & Toso is considered the island's oldest glass manufacturer. Since 2018, the palazzo on the banks of the Rio dei Vetrai has showcased a fairy-tale world of glass. The showpiece Taif, a massive chandelier designed in 1980 for the ruler of Saudi Arabia, is a true highlight. ***barovier.com***
Berengo Studio 1989 For over 30 years, Adriano Berengo has been pioneering new directions in glass art. In the spaces of an old factory, visitors can watch glass artists at work and admire pieces from the Glasstress 8 ½ Collection, created in collaboration with world-renowned artists such as Ai Weiwei, Thomas Schütte, and Tracey Emin. Fondamenta dei Vetrai 109/a, Tel. +39 041 73 94 53, open Monday to Sunday from 9:00 AM to 5:00 PM ***berengo.com***

SER
VICE

BACARI

Everywhere vegetable vendors, fishmongers, and craftsmen are at work – on bridges, around the Rialto Market, and near boat landings – you'll find the warm, intimate wine bars of the Venetians. Known as Bacari, named after Bacchus, the god of wine, some of these spots remain well-kept secrets, while others, despite their nondescript facades and weathered signs, have been discovered by visitors over the years. So much so that it is now possible to book a Giro di Ombra (Bacari tour) – fortunately in small groups, as the tiny spaces wouldn't allow for anything more. Traditionally, Bacari had almost no seating – perhaps a stool at the long bar, a chair in a corner, or a small bench outside the door. That hasn't changed much. The real focus remains the long counters lined with wine racks, where glass cases display delicious small bites perfect for a quick snack. Typical Cicchetti include Baccalà Mantecato (creamy salted cod on bread), Polpette (spiced meatballs), and Sarde in Saor (sweet-and-sour marinated sardines). Beyond these classics, each host offers their own specialties, from spiced tripe (Trippa) to veal cartilage with onions (Nerveti) to the so-called Paperini, triangular sandwiches sometimes filled with ox neck or pig's feet. Even more impressive than the variety of Cicchetti is the selection of wines, always served in small glasses known as Ombra – just 3.5 fl oz of ice-cold Prosecco, Pinot Grigio, or Riesling, alongside full-bodied reds like Merlot and Cabernet Sauvignon. One wine, Fragolino, a sweet variety with a strawberry-like aroma, is technically illegal to serve, as it falls below the minimum alcohol content of 11.5%. The term Ombra has its origins in the old wine sellers who used to set up mobile stalls in St. Mark's Square, constantly shifting into the shade (ombra) to keep their beverages cool. Around the Rialto Market, Bacari open early in the morning, but by 11 AM, locals are gathered, sipping an Ombra and nibbling on Cicchetti while catching up on the latest news. Those embarking on a self-guided Giro di Ombra will be delighted to find how easily their destinations can be located using Google Maps.

nutella

CANTINA DEL VINO GIÀ SCHIAVI

DORSODURO

Unlike the tiny Bacari tucked into the narrow streets near the Rialto Bridge, this historic wine bar, also known as Al Bottegon, is visible from afar along the banks of the Rio San Trovaso. Originally a wine shop, founded in 1944, its overflowing wine racks still bear witness to its roots. For 50 years, Alessandra de Rispinis has stood behind the counter alongside her sons, serving guests with a mix of charm and humor. She's famous not just for her stories but also for her exceptional selection of Cicchetti, which have people lining up before the doors even open. Throughout the years, she has tirelessly crafted new combinations using ingredients from the sea and the vegetable gardens of the lagoon. Her creations are documented in Cicchettario: The Legendary Recipes of Al Bottegon in Venice (dvb-mainz.de). Inside, space is limited, but the real magic happens outdoors – where guests gather on the steps of the Ponte San Trovaso, across from the church of the same name. And the Cicchetti? Expect delicate bites like Octopus Carpaccio with Celery, Brie with Oxheart Tomato and Anchovies, Mushrooms with Ricotta, Swordfish and Artichokes, or even more elaborate treats like Crostini with Squid Terrine, Orange Mayonnaise, and Ketchup. As for drinks, a glass of lightly fruity Valdobbiadene Prosecco, served ice cold, is the perfect refreshment. The shelves house an extensive selection of spirits and wines – whiskeys, malts, grappa, amaro, port, and sherry – alongside some of Italy's finest wines, from Antinori and Brunello di Montepulciano to Soave, Pinot Grigio, and Bianco di Custoza. Fondamenta Nani, Dorsoduro 992 Tel. +39 041-523 00 34 Open daily from 8:30 AM – 8:30 PM, closed Sundays and one week in August ***cantinaschiavi.com***

FOLPETI

BOILED BABY OCTOPUS

SERVES 4
42.2 lbs (1 kg) baby octopus, 2 bay leaves, 1 lemon (juice and zest), 1 chili pepper, 1 tbsp olive oil, 1 bunch flat-leaf parsley, chopped, Salt and pepper

PREPARATION
Ask your fishmonger to clean the octopus. Bring salted water to a boil with the bay leaves, half a lemon, and the chili pepper. Briefly dip the octopus into the boiling water so that the tentacles curl up. Then, fully submerge them and simmer for about 30 minutes. As they cool, mix olive oil, the remaining lemon juice, chopped parsley, salt, and pepper. Drizzle over the octopus and serve warm.

BISATO IN UMIDO

BRAISED EEL

SERVES 4
3 tbsp olive oil, 1 onion, finely chopped, 1 carrot, finely chopped, 1 celery stalk, finely chopped, 14 oz (400 g) eel, gutted and cut into pieces, ¾ cup (200 ml) white wine, 2 tomatoes, peeled, deseeded, and diced, Chopped basil leaves, Salt and pepper

PREPARATION
Heat the olive oil in a large pot and sauté the onion, carrot, and celery. Add the eel and sear briefly. Pour in the white wine and bring to a boil.
Reduce the heat and simmer for about 20 minutes until the eel is cooked through. Add the tomatoes and basil and cook for another 5 minutes.
Season with salt and pepper before serving.

SCAMPI BUSARA

SCAMPI IN WHITE WINE

SERVES 4
5 garlic cloves, finely chopped, 5 tbsp olive oil, 2.2 lbs (1 kg) scampi (peeled and deveined), 1.7 fl oz (¼ l) dry white wine, Salt, Sweet paprika, Chopped parsley, 0.7 oz (20 g) breadcrumbs

PREPARATION
Sauté the garlic in olive oil in a large pan, then remove the garlic cloves. Add the scampi and toss to coat. Pour in the white wine and cook over high heat until reduced. Season with salt and paprika, then sprinkle with parsley and breadcrumbs before serving, without sauce.

VERZE SOFEGAE

BRAISED SAVOY CABBAGE

SERVES 4
1 onion, finely chopped, 1 garlic clove, finely chopped, 2 tbsp olive oil, 2.2 lbs (1 kg) savoy cabbage, shredded, 1 sprig rosemary (needles only), Salt and pepper

PREPARATION
Sauté the onion and garlic in olive oil.
Add the shredded cabbage, salt, pepper, and rosemary.
Cover and simmer over low heat for about 90 minutes.
Remove the lid and cook for another 30 minutes.

SARDE IN SAOR

MARINATED SARDINES

SERVES 6

2.2 lbs (1 kg) fresh sardines, cleaned, washed, and patted dry, 7 oz (200 g) flour, 6 cups (1,5 l) sunflower oil (for frying), 1.5 qt olive oil, 3.3 lbs (1,5 kg) white onions, thinly sliced, 3.5 fl oz (100 ml) dry white wine, 1 handful raisins, 1 handful pine nuts, 2 bay leaves, Salt and pepper

PREPARATION

Dredge the sardines in flour. Fry them in hot sunflower oil until golden brown. Drain on paper towels and lightly salt. In a large pot, heat the remaining sunflower oil and olive oil. Sauté the onions over medium heat until translucent. Deglaze with white wine and reduce slightly. Add the raisins, pine nuts, salt, and pepper, and mix well. Place the cooled sardines in a large bowl, pour the hot onion marinade over them, and mix well. Cover and let sit at room temperature for at least 12 hours, preferably overnight.

INSALATA DI PIOVRA

OCTOPUS SALAD

SERVES 4

1 carrot, peeled and diced, 1 celery stalk, peeled and diced, 1 garlic clove, halved, 2 bay leaves, 2.2 lbs (1 kg) octopus, cleaned and washed, 1 oz (30 g) olive oil, 0.3 fl oz (10 ml) lemon juice, 1 handful parsley, chopped, Salt and pepper

PREPARATION

Bring a large pot of water to a boil. Add the carrot, celery, garlic, and bay leaves.Season with salt and pepper. Once boiling, dip the octopus tentacle tips into the water to curl them, then fully submerge the octopus. Cover and simmer over low heat for about 45 minutes. Remove the octopus from the water and let it cool. Meanwhile, mix the olive oil, lemon juice, chopped parsley, salt, and pepper for the dressing. Cut the octopus into bite-sized pieces and toss with the dressing.

POLPETTE DI TONNO

TUNA MEATBALLS

SERVES 4

1 slice of toast (soaked in a little milk), 10.5 oz (300 g) boiled potatoes, mashed, Chopped parsley, 1 egg, 1 small handful arugula, torn, 7 oz (200 g) canned tuna in oil, drained, 1.4 oz (40 g) Taggiasca olives, chopped, Breadcrumbs, Olive oil for drizzling, Salt and pepper

PREPARATION

Soak the bread in milk. Mix the mashed potatoes with the soaked bread, parsley, egg, arugula, and tuna. Add the olives and season with salt and pepper. Form small balls and roll them in breadcrumbs. Place them on a baking sheet lined with parchment paper, drizzle with a little olive oil, and bake in a preheated oven at 400°F for about 20 minutes.

FIORI DI ZUCCA E BACCALÀ

ZUCCHINI BLOSSOMS WITH SALT COD

SERVES 20

17.5 oz (500 g) salt cod, dried and soaked, 8.5 fl oz (200 ml) milk, 2 garlic cloves, 2 bay leaves, Olive oil, 20 zucchini blossoms, Peanut oil (for frying), 3.5 fl oz (100 ml) beer, 3.5 fl oz (100 ml) oil, 3.5 oz (100 g) flour, 1 egg white

PREPARATION

Simmer the salt cod in milk with garlic and bay leaves for 30 minutes. Remove from heat, discard the garlic and bay leaves, and mash the salt cod with a little olive oil until creamy. Clean the zucchini blossoms, removing the stems. Fill with the salt cod mixture. For the batter, whisk together the beer, oil, flour, and egg white until smooth. Dip the filled zucchini blossoms into the batter, ensuring they are fully coated. Fry in hot peanut oil until golden brown. Drain on paper towels and serve with a glass of wine or beer.

CANTINA DO SPADE

SAN POLO

The inscription on the wall says it all: "Vinum bonum fortificat cor hominis" – a good wine strengthens the human heart. The history of this rather unassuming establishment, hidden at the end of a dark alley, dates back to the 15th century. Carlo de Zuane, the first innkeeper of this cozy tavern, became a member of the Venetian innkeepers' guild in 1488. Later, city records show that in 1566, the Fiscari family leased the tavern, then known as Osteria delle do Spade, to a certain Battista. The old wooden bridge at this location was replaced by a steel bridge in 1886. The most famous guest was undoubtedly Casanova, who is said to have merrily indulged here in 1744. A small side room is named in his honor. Otherwise, the interior has a rustic Alpine feel, with the usual dominating counter at its center, a few small tables inside, and a wooden bench outside. A large chalkboard, leaning against an old wine barrel, announces the daily specials. Beyond the liquid refreshments, the menu features an excellent selection of Paperini – bite-sized sandwiches filled with stockfish mousse or tuna paste – along with savory meatballs, ham croquettes, and more traditional delicacies like stuffed pig's trotters, headcheese, or salsice di secole, sausages made from beef vertebrae. Classic favorites include fried zucchini blossoms and spicy meatballs. Popular wines include Raboso and Malbec from the Piave Valley, as well as Campofiorin from the Masi winery. The Spritz, typically mixed with Aperol, Campari, Bitter, or Select, is served at Do Spade with Centino, a liqueur from the 1950s. For those wanting a deeper dive into Venetian cuisine, the tavern offers cooking classes on Wednesdays and Fridays from 11 AM to 2 PM, combined with a guided shopping tour at the nearby Rialto Market.
Calle do Spade, San Polo 859, Tel. 041-521 05 83, open daily from 10:00 AM to 3:00 PM and from 6:00 PM to 10:00 PM,***cantinadospade.com***

CANTINA DO MORI

When talking about Bacari in Venice, one of the oldest names that comes up is Cantina do Mori, a wine bar that has been documented as early as 1462. Located near the Rialto Bridge, it has long been a favorite haunt of fishmongers, fruit and vegetable sellers, goldsmiths, and gondoliers. Especially in the warm summer months, a carafe of ice-cold Prosecco is always on the counter. The selection also includes a variety of still and sparkling wines – both Spumante and Frizzante – along with an ever-expanding list of wine labels. Some local wines still arrive weekly in large demijohns, contributing to the charming, old-world atmosphere alongside the copper pots hanging from the ceiling. Many of the dishes that were once served in bowls and platters behind the glass counter are now offered as topped baguette slices, spread with salt cod mousse, fresh cheese-pistachio cream, or topped with the classic Sarde in Saor and marinated herring. Calle Do Mori, San Polo 429 Tel. +39 041-522 54 01 Open Mon–Fri 8:00 AM – 8:00 PM, Sat until 3:00 PM, closed Sundays.

BAR ALL 'ARCO

This rustic little corner bar near the Rialto Market is only open in the morning. Francesco Pinto and his son Matteo follow a strict market-to-table principle in selecting their delicate small plates. Everything the Venetian-born chef does, he does with passion. There are no tables – everything happens at the bar. Expect an excellent selection of Tramezzini, including those filled with truffle and cream cheese or tuna paste. Or try toasted white bread with salami and figs, paired with a wide wine selection or a classic Spritz. If you ask about the recipes for his creations, Francesco is more than happy to share. On sunny days, a few tables are set up outside. Calle dell'Occhialer, San Polo 436 Tel. +39 041-520 56 66 Open daily 10:00 AM – 2:30 PM, closed Wednesdays

OSTERIA AL SQUERO

The best seat is outside, overlooking the historic 17th-century gondola workshop across the canal. At the counter, you'll find an enticing variety of Cicchetti, including crostini with salmon, pink pepper, and lemon, as well as combinations like tuna and olives or speck and mushrooms. In addition to wine and Spritz, the café also serves an excellent espresso. Fondamenta Nani, Dorsoduro 943 Tel. +39 335 600 75 13 Open Tue–Sun 10:00 AM – 9:30 PM, closed Mondays

ANTICO DOLO

With its red facade and many windows, this 15th-century building once stood in the heart of Venice's old red-light district. Some believe it was once a brothel. Today, the walls are decorated with photos of distinguished guests, and records show that it also operated as a Tripperia, specializing in offal dishes, before Bruno Ruffini turned it into a wine bar in 1989. His son Matteo now runs it, and the menu still features tripa rissa, a classic Venetian offal dish cooked with herbs, and Castradina, slow-braised mutton with onions and garlic. These pair well with a glass of Orto di Venezia from Sant'Erasmo island. For newcomers, the Degustazione di Cicchetti offers a tasting selection for €20. In recent years, the bar has expanded to include a few tables where refined Venetian cuisine is served at higher prices. Local favorites include Bigoli in Salsa (whole wheat pasta with anchovies and onions), Pastisso (a seasonal vegetable lasagna), and Maltagliati with scallops or tuna carpaccio. Ruga Rialto, San Polo 778 Tel. +39 041-522 65 46 Open daily 11:00 AM – midnight

AL PROSECCO

A favorite among locals. Children play under the shade of large trees, dog walkers pass by, and housewives park their shopping carts to sit for an obligatory chat on the terrace. Brothers Stefano and Davide Corrò serve up beautiful platters of cold cuts, cheeses, and hams in their wood-paneled tavern, accompanied by a vast selection of Prosecco and over 600 wine labels, including many organic wines. On Saturdays, the menu features fresh oysters or fish carpaccio. Campo San Giacomo dell'Orio, Santa Croce 1503 Tel. +39 041-524 02 22 Open daily 9:00 AM – 9:00 PM, closed Sundays and August

ENOTECA AL VOLTO

In 1936, Gigi Carbon opened an Osteria here. His son Carlo transformed it into a wine bar in the 1950s, quickly gaining a reputation beyond the city. Even the legendary wine critic Luigi Veronelli took notice, and the Missoni fashion dynasty became loyal patrons. Countless wine labels now adorn the ceiling, a testament to the passion of current owner Giancarlo Mersini, who has curated a collection of over 1,000 bottles, predominantly Italian, followed by French and other international selections. Among the best Cicchetti here: baked mussels, salmon sandwiches with egg, and Pecetti alla Greca (anchovies marinated in olive oil, vinegar, and capers). The bar now offers a few tables where guests can enjoy simple Venetian dishes. Calle Cavalli, San Marco 4081 Tel. +39 041-522 89 45 Open daily 10:00 AM – 4:00 PM and 6:00 PM – 10:00 PM

AL MERCA

The small bench outside fills up quickly, and guests happily gather in groups on Campo Bella Vienna, holding a glass of wine and a plate of Cicchetti in hand. The wine bar is simple, the panini are flavorful, and the prices are reasonable. San Polo 213 Open Mon–Sat 10:00 AM – 2:30 PM and 6:00 PM – 9:00 PM (Fri & Sat until 9:30 PM), closed Sun-

MADE IN VENICE

GIBERTO

Giberto Arrivabene has lived since childhood in the enchanting world of Palazzo Papadopoli, surrounded by his family and frescoes by Tiepolo. With his wife Bianca and their five children residing on the top floor, the rest of the house and its tranquil garden were taken over in 2014 by the luxurious city hideaway Aman Venice. His passion for glass art has accompanied him since childhood. Whenever a glass broke in his family home, he would set off for Murano to find a suitable replacement. Along the way, he watched the glass masters at work – craftsmen whose numbers have dwindled significantly since then – and soon ventured into creating his own pieces. The result speaks for itself: an extraordinary collection of glasses, sculptures, and other designs, always evolving with new ideas. To his great delight, the spring of 2024 brought the opportunity to open a Giberto shop in one of the coveted spaces on the Rialto Bridge. With the help of architect Giovanni Rubin de Cervin Albrizzi, he was able to showcase his carefully curated glass objects in the perfect light. "We are living in challenging times," he says. "The shortage of skilled artisans and ever-rising production costs weigh heavily on us, as do the countless counterfeits over which we have no control."

Incidentally, his two eldest children have inherited both his love for beautiful things and his business acumen. Under the logo VIBI Venezia, they design and produce their own collection of Furlane.

Giberto Venezia, Ponte di Rialto 2, San Polo 1364, Tel. 041-277 00 86, ***giberto.it***

FAVORITE SPOTS OF GIBERTO ARRIVABENE

I have been a regular at Trattoria alla Madonna for years, a restaurant under the Rialto Bridge that has preserved its Venetian character, with an atmosphere that makes me feel at home. I often went there with my father, which makes it even more meaningful to me. Just a short walk from the Rialto Market, it guarantees freshness and quality. I also enjoy going to Osteria Il Milion, in Corte del Milion, which belongs to my friend Roberto. Imagine – the thought that Marco Polo was born in this very house. It is a place that is one hundred percent Venetian, radiating warmth and a sense of belonging. It will always have a place in my heart.

And of course, there is Harry's Bar, a true institution in the city. I deeply admire how it has managed to preserve its original spirit for so many years.

Trattoria alla Madonna, Calle della Madonna 594, San Polo, Tel. 041-522 38 24 Osteria Il Milion, San Giovanni Crisostomo, Tel. 041-522 93 02 Harry's Bar (see p. 229)

FORTUNY

When one thinks of Rubelli, fabrics immediately come to mind, while Fortuny is synonymous with its often teardrop-shaped, unmistakable lamps. Designing and creating them was one of the many talents of the Spanish artist Mariano Fortuny. Born in Granada in 1871, he was immersed in the Moorish fairy-tale world of Andalusia from an early age, which fueled his imagination. It was only natural that in 1889, he moved to Venice with his wife Henriette, never leaving the city again. Together, they took their first steps in the world of fashion – he designed dresses and scarves, while she experimented with colors and various printing techniques. They lived and worked in the Palazzo Pesaro degli Orfei and were happy.
His keen interest in advancing stage lighting led to a series of groundbreaking lighting designs. When Mariano passed away in 1949, Henriette sold both the production facilities on Giudecca and the exclusive rights to Fortuny's cotton fabrics and wallpapers. For a few years, she continued working with velvet and silk textiles in Palazzo Orfei, but eventually, her husband's artistic legacy faded into the background. Fortuny was rediscovered in 1975 when the Palazzo Fortuny was established as a house museum in the Piano Nobile of the Palazzo Pesaro degli Orfei, offering a beautiful cross-section of the Spaniard's artistic life – photography, painting, sculpture, lighting technology, and fashion design. It would take a few more years before the enchanting world of this Spanish polymath was revived by the curiosity and passion of Venetian artisan Lino Lando. His primary focus was on reproducing Fortuny's original lamps, including the 1909 Studio collection, paying tribute to the legendary stage lighting designs. He also brought back the signature pleated fabrics that, during Fortuny's lifetime, were crafted into elegant, figure-hugging dresses, once hanging in the wardrobes of Peggy Guggenheim and Eleonora Duse. The turning point came in 1984 with the perfection of the pleating technique. Since then, Lino Lando has been producing silk kimonos, kaftans, dresses, and scarves inspired by the Far East, along with cushions and curtains. A true feast for the senses, Fortuny's iconic oriental silk lamps can be found not only in restaurants and hotels across Venice but also around the world. Fortuny now has two stores in Venice and additional locations in Paris and Munich. Dorsoduro 180/A, Tel. 041-521 01 87, open daily from 10:00 AM to 6:30 PM San Marco 2428, Tel. 041-520 05 05, open daily from 10:00 AM to 6:30 PM, fortuny.de The museum spaces, damaged during the 2019 flood, have since been restored.
Palazzo Fortuny, San Marco 3958, Tel. 041-520 09 95, ***fortuny.visitmuve.it***

FAVORITE SPOTS OF LINO LANDO:

There are two museums in the city that continuously serve as sources of inspiration for me. One is Palazzo Fortuny, which captivated me from a young age, back when Fortuny's widow, Henriette, still lived in the palazzo. The other is the Museum of Oriental Art on the top floor of Ca' Pesaro, a hidden gem largely untouched by mass tourism. Particularly remarkable is the precious collection of Enrico di Borbone, Conte di Bardi, who undertook numerous journeys to China, Japan, and Indonesia in the late 19th century. (see p. 143)

BEVILACQUA

The Bevilacqua family's roots trace back to 1499. In the 19th century, Luigi Bevilacqua took over a number of looms from the Venetian silk guild and established his own weaving workshop. Initially located in the Sestiere Castello, the company has been housed in Palazzo Labia in Santa Croce, right on the Grand Canal, since 1918. Today, the business is run by Dottore Alberto Bevilacqua and his brother Rodolfo, the fourth generation of the family to carry on the tradition. Their challenge is to create ever-new patterns on the historic looms, producing textiles for churches, theaters, hotels, Venetian palazzi, and haute couture fashion houses. A visit to the workshop – available as a guided tour – is a journey into the past. Towering shelves hold thousands of unused punch cards, and the historic Jacquard looms appear like relics from another era. Five skilled artisans operate the looms manually, guiding the shuttles by hand, cutting the threads with a blade, and pressing the foot pedals. One of the most valuable fabrics produced here is the Soprarizzo velvet, a high-pile textile woven through an exceptionally labor-intensive process. Due to its complexity, only 12 to 16 inches can be produced per day. Campiello de la Comare, Santa Croce 1320 Tel. +39 041-72 15 66 Open Mon–Fri 9:30 AM – 1:30 PM & 2:30 PM – 5:00 PM, Sat by appointment, closed Sundays Showroom & shop: Campo di Santa Maria del Giglio, San Marco 2520, ***luigi-bevilacqua.com***

ATTILO CODOGNATO

Just a few steps from Harry's Bar, the gleaming storefront of Attilio Codognato speaks for itself: Venice's most famous jeweler is dedicated to the dark, mysterious side of his city. His eccentric creations feature skulls on rings, snakes wrapped around bracelets, and miniature coffins as delicate pendants, all adorned with dazzling gemstones. In a way, his designs reflect Venice itself – delicate yet powerful, opulent yet perpetually at risk of disappearing. His clientele speaks volumes: Andy Warhol, Luchino Visconti, the Duke and Duchess of Windsor, and Maria Callas have all been customers. Like Arrigo Cipriani, who at 92 still runs Harry's Bar just two doors down, Attilio Codognato, now 94, is one of Venice's last true icons. He insists on personally assisting every customer, following the family tradition of offering bespoke consultations.

His commitment to exclusivity is so strong that he famously rejected an offer to open a New York boutique. Walking into his shop feels like stepping back in time – very little has changed since his great-grandfather Simeone Codognato founded it in 1866. Unfortunately, there is no heir to take over: his son is a museum curator in Naples, and his daughter is a psychotherapist in London. Calle Vallaresso, San Marco 1316 Tel. +39 333 188 94 63 ***attilocodognato.it***

RUBELLI

When Lorenzo Rubelli founded the company at the end of the 19th century, he could not have imagined that Rubelli would become a global brand four generations later. A look into the company archives or the collection of the Fondazione Rubelli, founded in 2018 by Alessandro Favoretto Rubelli, offers insight into how Rubelli has evolved from a traditional weaving mill into a modern enterprise. The design of approximately 5000 fabric patterns has involved international artists such as Guido Cadorin and Gió Ponti. Among the collection are opulent brocades woven from historical designs, damasks with generous rose motifs, and velvets intricately worked with gold and silk, including an Altobasso velvet from the 16th century, once used to craft the stoles of the procurators. The foundation also holds exceptional pieces from Asia, America, and Africa that have been donated to its collection. Representing the fifth generation, Nicolò Favoretto Rubelli is responsible for the international market. Beyond its fabrics, the Rubelli portfolio includes the Rubelli Casa collection and a collaboration with Armani Casa. Examples of the brand's widespread presence include Rubelli fabrics in the recently renovated interiors of the Gritti, in Castello del Nero on Lake Como, in the new suites of the Venice Simplon-Orient-Express, in the Albertina in Vienna, and at La Scala in Milan. After the most recent fire at Teatro La Fenice, Rubelli donated fabrics for its restoration. Production takes place on 31 electronic Jacquard looms at the company's own weaving facility on Lake Como. The foundation is located in Palazzo Ca' Pisani Rubelli, sharing the space with the showroom, shop, and family residence. San Marco 3393, Tel. 041-523 61 10, ***rubelli.com***

NICOLÒ FAVORETTO RUBELLI'S FAVORITE SPOT

"Lineadombra is one of the city's hidden gems, not far from Chiesa della Salute. As a child, I used to escape school and hide there – it was just a simple bar back then.
Now, it has transformed into a stylish, modern restaurant serving contemporary Venetian cuisine. The wine list is extensive, like a thick catalog. Sitting there on a sunny day, watching the boats pass by on the Giudecca Canal – I can't imagine anything more romantic." (p. 168)

LATE NIGHT SECRETS

L.P.V. BAR

With the complete renovation of Hotel Londra Palace, its legendary bar also received a new look in 2024. Since this refined establishment took its place alongside the prestigious Danieli and Metropole in 1853, it has added to the parade of grand hotels along the Riva degli Schiavoni. The bar has become a kind of pilgrimage site for cocktail aficionados. In 2019, bartender Marino Lucchetti's creation was named Martini Cocktail of the Year. Popular choices include Margaritas, Marinos, Mojitos, and rosé wines. For summer, guests enjoy Bellinis with fresh peach purée, Rossinis with strawberries, or Puccinis with mandarin. To accompany the drinks: Club Sandwich, Caesar Salad, Caprese, or Prosciutto with melon. Riva degli Schiavoni, Castello 4171, Tel. 041-620 05 33, ***relaischateaux.com***

ORIENTAL BAR & BISTRO

Among the many beloved cocktail bars of Venice's traditional five-star hotels, both the bar at Hotel Metropole and the hotel itself truly deserve the title of a "Cabinet of Curiosities." Over generations, the Beggiato family has gathered beautiful objects from around the world – not only carefully selected antiques but also exquisite collections ranging from calling card holders to precious fans.

The very thought that the space where cocktails are now served was once, in 1686, the oratory where Vivaldi gave music lessons is enough to make many dream. Two hundred years later, the hotel's history began, first as Casa Kirsch and later as Hotel Metropole, welcoming devoted guests such as Marcel Proust, Thomas Mann, and Sigmund Freud. In 2017, neon artist Joseph Kosuth created a special piece for the bar, paying homage to that bygone era. The Oriental Bar remains a truly unique place: guests sit under the soft glow of Fortuny lamps, sinking into deep red velvet, choosing from 43 varieties of gin, signature drinks like the Campari Fresh, and classic cocktails with a creative twist, accompanied by small appetizers or the Metropole Cheeseburger. Riva degli Schiavoni, Castello 4149, Tel. +39 041 520 50 44, open daily from 12:00 to 24:00, ***hotelmetropole.com***

EXPERIMENTAL COCKTAIL CLUB

When this boutique hotel opened in 2018 in a former shipping company headquarters on the Zattere, it faced immediate challenges – a catastrophic flood, then the pandemic.

But today, this Dorsoduro hotspot is thriving again. Guests sip Aperitifs on the terrace overlooking the Giudecca, lounge in the garden, or enjoy the New York-inspired bardesigned by Cristina Celestino. The team behind Experimental – also present in Ibiza, Menorca, and Paris – first made their name with bars, and their mixologists continue to push boundaries. A few steps away, their Bistro Adriatico serves some of the best tapas in the city.Fondamenta Zattere al Ponte Lungo, Dorsoduro 1410 Tel. +39 041 098 02 00 Open 6:30 PM – 1:00 AM (Fri & Sat until 2:00 AM), closed Tuesday & Wednesday, ***experimentalgroup.com***

IL MERCANTE

With the Basilica dei Frari as its backdrop, Alessandro Zampieri has built a reputation for crafting some of Venice's most creative cocktails. This historic space has served many roles – once part of city administration, later a brothel in 1870, and for a time, a café. Today, it retains its historic charm while pushing mixology to new heights. Zampieri's cocktails feature exotic, innovative ingredients, inspired by the adventures of Marco Polo, Magellan, and Sir Francis Drake. One standout: "Silk", a blend of seaweed distillate, green rooibos tea, cherry, cardamom, kefir, lime leaves, and verjus. Campo dei Frari, San Polo 2564 Tel. +39 041 476 73 05 Open Mon–Wed 6:00 PM – 12:30 AM, Fri until 1:00 AM, Sat & Sun 10:30 AM – 4:30 PM & 6:00 PM – midnight

LIBRARY BAR

The opening of Hotel Nolinski Venezia in 2024 in the former stock exchange building drew significant attention with its eclectic blend of Liberty, Modernism, Mid-Century, and numerous contemporary artworks spread across five floors. Just a short distance from the reception, on the third floor, guests will find the Library Bar, named for the more than 4,000 books lining the walls of this intimate establishment. Despite its size, there is also space for a piano and plush red velvet seating areas. The ten-meter-high ceiling, adorned with a stunning underwater scene, was painted by artist and actor Simon Buret. At the bar, the magic happens in the hands of award-winning mixologist Jérémy Bacquet, who has been the creative director behind all bar concepts of the Evok Hotel Group for years. One of his signature cocktails is the "Gritti," a blend of Pisco, pomegranate juice, jasmine syrup, lime juice, and soda.

For the hotel's fine-dining restaurant, Greek chef Philip Chronopoulos leads the kitchen.

Calle Larga XXII Marzo, San Marco 2032, Tel. +39 041 406 24 59, open daily from 17:30 to 00:30, ***nolinskivenezia.com***

TAVERNA LA FENICE

It doesn't get much closer to Teatro La Fenice than this. Known as a restaurant since 1860, the venue is particularly famous for its American Bar, which stays open late into the night. A glance while passing by reveals comfortable vintage armchairs, small tables, and potted plants on the terrace, with regular guests including theater professionals and their audience. Perfect for an aperitivo before or after a performance or simply as an after-dinner destination. Guests celebrating a special occasion sometimes indulge in rare treasures from the wine cellar, such as a bottle of Château Latour 1995 for €3,250 or a sparkling Perrier-Jouët Belle Époque Blanc de Blanc 2004 for €1,150. Campiello Marinoni o de la Fenice, San Marco 1939, Tel. +39 041 522 38 56, open daily from 12:00 to 24:00.

TARNOWSKA'S AMERICAN BAR

The dark wooden paneling at this bar comes from Teatro La Fenice, but its infamous reputation stems from the Russian Countess Maria Tarnowska, whose lover Kamarowsky was murdered here – a scandal that made headlines across Europe. Today, inside the Hotel Ala, the bar remains a classic stop for a Bellini, Spritz, or Prosecco. Campo Santa Maria del Giglio, San Marco 2494 Tel. +39 041 520 83 33, ***hotelala.it***

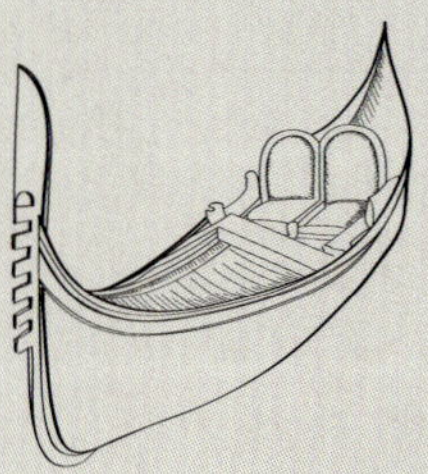

EXPE-RIENCES

INCONTRI CULTURALI

Venetian Dr. Manuela Zardo, who has had a second home and office in Munich for many years, organizes private small-group Venice tours on special themes, from the carnival classic Il Carnevale dei Veneziani with ball attendance to Biennale trips and the Festa del Redentore. Her Venice of the Venetians tour takes participants on long walks to hidden spots, presenting rare art treasures and telling mysterious stories, such as those about the once-powerful monastic orders or the lives of her favorite painters, Bellini and Titian. Franz-Joseph-Str. 41, 80801 Munich, Tel. 089 271 65 60, ***incontri.de***

GONDEL FAHREN

For heaven's sake, don't do anything that instantly marks you as a tourist! Some hesitate to book a gondola ride to maintain their bella figura, but that's nonsense. Gondolas belong to Venice, just as horse-drawn carriages belong to Vienna or Cinquecento tours to Rome. Today, gondolas are a tourist attraction, but they were once an essential mode of transport and a status symbol for wealthy Venetians – after all, in the 16th century, there were no fewer than 10,000 gondolas on the canals. Likewise, numerous boatyards were needed to build them. Today, only about 500 remain, and the number of boatyards can be counted on one hand. About eleven meters long and weighing 500 kilograms, a gondola consists of around 280 individual parts. Those interested in how they are built or repaired can visit the renowned Squero di San Trovaso in the Dorsoduro district, where gondola makers can be seen at work (squerosantrovaso.com). The city's best private guides organize tours, including Luisella Romeo, who also offers rowing tours and lessons, Tel. +39 349 084 83 03, ***seevenice.it***

MOTOR-SEGLER EDIPO RE

A highly comfortable and culinary-driven way to explore the lagoon and Venice's canals. Originally, this charming yacht belonged to a friend of Roman director Pier Paolo Pasolini. It had long been forgotten before being revived by Sibylle Righetti and Enrico Vianello. Soon, artists, writers, and musicians were once again coming on board, and now the historic motor sailer is available for tours. As one of the last fishermen on the island of Pellestrina, Enrico's father ensures a supply of freshly caught fish and seafood, served to a maximum of ten guests during a lagoon cruise. Everything else on the menu is sourced locally according to the zero-kilometer principle from regional producers. ***edipore.it***

FOR A BELLINI AT HARRY'S BAR

Giuseppe Cipriani, who grew up in the Black Forest as the son of an Italian guest worker family, left his mark on the city's history in his own way. At the end of the 1920s, he was a bartender at the Hotel Europa when he used his savings to help a young American, Harry Pickering, settle his hotel bill. Harry returned with enough dollars to open Harry's Bar with his new friend in May 1931 in an old warehouse at the end of Calle Vallaresso, which remains one of the world's most famous bars to this day. Writers, artists, Hollywood stars, and royals felt at home here thanks to Giuseppe's warmth and his modesty in dealing with people and life itself. In 1936, he bought an inn without electricity on Torcello, where Ernest Hemingway spent the winter of 1948/49 hunting ducks and writing Across the River and Into the Trees. Around the same time, Giuseppe invented the Bellini, a sparkling mix of white peach purée and Prosecco. The now world-famous summer drink was named after the striking red and pink tones in the paintings of Venetian artist Giovanni Bellini. The Locanda Cipriani, with its six guest rooms and excellent cuisine, is now a perfect hideaway for honeymooners.

Over the years, Giuseppe expanded his carefully curated portfolio with two more addresses, both on the island of Giudecca: Hotel Cipriani, with its lush garden and the city's largest pool, and Harry's Dolci, a haven for guests with a sweet tooth. Incidentally, guests boarding the nostalgic Venice Simplon-Orient-Express to London in the morning prefer to spend the night at what is now the Belmond Cipriani Hotel. One moment that will always be remembered is the day Giuseppe, following the diet instructions of Countess Mocenigo, sliced a delicate piece of beef into wafer-thin pieces and topped it with a light mousseline of mayonnaise, milk, Worcestershire sauce, lemon juice, and white pepper. The red and white tones in the paintings of Venetian history painter Vittore Carpaccio inspired the dish's name. Today, Carpaccio is not only a classic on the Harry's Bar menu, but the term has also become synonymous worldwide with anything served raw and sliced paper-thin, from scallops to beetroot. When Arrigo Cipriani, who still mingles with guests daily at over 90 years old, took over the bar from his father in 1980, he called it "a brilliant blend of luxury and simplicity" and decided to reveal the recipes for legendary dishes like Carpaccio, Risotto Primavera, and Club Sandwich in Harry's Bar Cookbook (Heyne Verlag Munich). A visit to the bar is a must for visitors to Venice, whether for a Bellini at the bar, a Carpaccio, or one of the other legendary dishes like Risotto Primavera, Giuseppe Cipriani's favorite.

Harry's Bar, Calle Vallaresso, San Marco 1323, Tel. +39 041 528 57 77, open daily from 11:00 AM to 11:00 PM; Locanda Cipriani, Torcello, Tel. +39 041 73 01 50, locandacipriani.com; Belmond Hotel Cipriani, Giudecca, Tel. +39 041 24 08 01, Belmond.com; Harry's Dolci, Giudecca, Fondamenta S. Biagio 773, Tel. +39 041 522 48 44, open from 12:00 PM to 11:00 PM, closed Mondays and Tuesdays; Venice Simplon-Orient-Express, booking via ***belmond.com***

TOP EVENTS

FILM FESTIVAL

The rather unremarkable Lido gained international recognition thanks to Thomas Mann's literary masterpiece "Death in Venice," especially after the story of the disillusioned composer Gustav von Aschenbach was brought to the screen in 1971, starring Dirk Bogarde in Luchino Visconti's adaptation. Filming took place, among other locations, in the salons of the Grand Hotel des Bains, where Mann had penned his novel. Today, the building has been converted into an apartment complex. The second, even more striking grand hotel is the Excelsior Palace, with its oriental-inspired facade. On its terrace in 1932, as part of the Art Biennale, the first Venice Film Festival was inaugurated with the screening of "Dr. Jekyll and Mr. Hyde," based on Robert Louis Stevenson's novel, followed by a grand ball. The glamour of the past may have faded, but today, one can still see Hollywood's biggest names on the international jury and walking the iconic red carpet. In 1937, the Palazzo del Cinema was built, and today, along with the Palazzo del Casinò and Sala Giardino, it remains the primary venue for the festival, which continues to be one of the world's most important film festivals, alongside Cannes and the Berlinale. ***labiennale.org***

BIENNALE

King Umberto I inaugurated the first Biennale in the spring of 1895. Of the 258 artists invited, half were Italian. Today, the Biennale has become a powerhouse of the international art scene. Its heart beats in the Giardini of the Castello district, where more than 30 national pavilions designed by renowned architects have been built and redesigned over time. In 1980, the Architecture Biennale was introduced and has since alternated every two years with the Art Biennale. labiennale.org. A recent addition to Venice's cultural calendar, Homo Faber, launched in 2022 by the Michelangelo Foundation, is an engaging forum for contemporary craftsmanship, hosted at the Giorgio Cini Foundation on the island of San Giorgio Maggiore.

CARNEVAL DI VENEZIA

André Malraux once remarked about the Carnival: "The fact that Venice lived longer than any other city in a constant festival and died masked makes it so interesting." Venetians have always loved masquerades, transformation, role reversal, mystery, and excess. As early as the Middle Ages, they organized masked balls and took things to such an extreme that Napoleon, in 1797, linked the fall of the Serenissima with the ban on Carnival. Venetians simply moved their passion for disguise into private societies, and it wasn't until the 1970s, when it was rediscovered as a tourist attraction, that the Carnival regained momentum. The strategy clearly worked. Every year, ten days before Ash Wednesday, the season of masks and grand balls begins. Venetians and visitors alike turn the area around St. Mark's Square into a catwalk of vanity. The bakeries and cafés are filled with the scent of cinnamon and raisins, as the fluffy Carnival fritters, known as Fritelle, make their appearance. The most famous and dazzling of all masked balls is the "Ballo del Doge," organized for over twenty years by costume designer and society queen Antonia Sautter. Guests from around the world book the ball, which rivals the Vienna Opera Ball in terms of decor, including dinner and a show. They arrive in Venice in time to select their historical costumes, complete with headpieces and masks, from Antonia Sautter's vast collection (Calle del Carro, San Marco 1628, Tel. 041-523 26 62, antoniasautter.it). The number one name in mask-making is "Ca'Macana," which has also supplied Hollywood productions, including the masks for Lasse Hallström's "Casanova" and Stanley Kubrick's "Eyes Wide Shut." Workshops are available for those who wish to create their own mask (Calle delle Botteghe, Dorsoduro 3172, Tel. 041-520 32 29, camacana.com). Among the most popular costume tailors is the handpicked team at Atelier Pietro Longhi (San Polo 2454, Tel. 041-71 44 78, pietrolonghi.com). The Carnival ends on Ash Wednesday with the Concerti dell Ceneri and a grand fireworks display. ***carnevale.venezia.it***

VAGA LONGA

Established in 1975 as a protest against the increasing number of motorboats in the lagoon, this popular rowing marathon takes place on Pentecost Sunday. Boats of all kinds gather in St. Mark's Basin before heading north toward the lagoon islands. The route passes through Burano and Mazzorbo before looping back through Murano, the Cannaregio Canal, and the entire length of the Grand Canal to Punta della Dogana, marking the race's finish. ***valalonga.eu***

REDENTORE

The joyous festival marking the end of the devastating plague epidemic of 1577 remains the highlight of Venice's annual calendar. On the day before the third Saturday in July, a wooden pontoon bridge is constructed from Zattere to the island of Giudecca, where the Church of the Redeemer stands. The festivities begin on Friday evening, as a procession of small boats, including numerous gondolas, makes its way toward the basin of St. Mark's. The grand fireworks display remains the spectacular centerpiece of the event. On Saturday, Venetians make a pilgrimage to the Redentore Church, lighting candles in remembrance. Those without a boat or an invitation aboard a friend's can rent one from "Brussa is Boat" (brussaisboat.it) or book a spot on the Redentore Suite at the Gritti Hotel, where the terrace accommodates up to 100 guest (***marriott.com***).

REGATA STORICA

Owning a boat is a symbol of freedom for Venetians, many of whom are members of traditional rowing clubs that organize prominent races throughout the year. The Regata Storica, the most dazzling of all, has taken place annually on the first Sunday in September since 1899. During the event, Vaporetto service is temporarily suspended, and the palazzi along the Grand Canal are adorned with colorful flags. The grand sporting and social event begins with a historic gondola parade, led by a replica of the Bucintoro, the most magnificent of all gondolas, once reserved for the Doge. Securing a front-row seat on one of the city's most exclusive terraces becomes a fierce competition among concierges of the luxury hotels. The regatta, which features various types of boats, starts at the Giardini in Castello and spans the entire four kilometers of the Grand Canal to Ca' Foscari. One of the three race categories is traditionally reserved for female rowers. The final event is the highly anticipated gondola race, in which two rowers in historical costumes compete. The winners are awarded honorary banners. ***regatastoricavenezia.it***

FESTA DELLA MADONNA DELLA SALUTE

The last major festival of the year, celebrated annually on November 21, commemorates the end of the plague epidemic of 1630-31, which claimed a quarter of the city's population, including the great painter Titian. At the time, Doge Nicolò Contarini organized a prayer procession for all survivors and vowed to build a church in honor of the Virgin Mary. Designed by the young Baldassare Longhena, the Basilica took over 50 years to complete and is now one of the city's architectural icons at the entrance to the Grand Canal. Much like the Redentore Festival, a pontoon bridge is built for the occasion, this time connecting the Vaporetto station at Santa Maria del Giglio across the Grand Canal to the Salute landing. Thousands of Venetians take part in the annual procession, and the church remains open from 5:45 AM to 10:30 PM on that day. Traditionally, the dish served is Castradina, a hearty mutton stew.

INDEX

A

Acquadelle in sauce **134**
Artichokes with mullet roe **176**

B

Baked cuttlefish in saor with black fregula sarda, bisque, and celeriac **124**
Bigoli with shrimp, fresh artichokes, and cherry tomatoes **203**
Bottoni with Vicenza-style stockfish, baby squid, and lovage **34**
Braised quail with chestnuts and radicchietti **112**
Braised veal cheeks with coffee and broccoli-celery millefoglie **172**
Braised savoy cabbage **217**

C

Cappelletti with Parmesan, black truffle, lobster, and lobster broth **90**
Ceviche of golden mullet **94**
Cippamisu – a variation of the classic tiramisu **184**
Crispy phyllo crackers with beef carpaccio **54**

D

Deep-fried Moeche with purple Sant'Erasmo artichokes **97**
Deep-fried sea bass fillet Mediterranean style with broccoli rabe and katsuobushi **152**

E

Eggplant garden from Sant'Erasmo **28**

F

Fennel cream soup with parsnip, goat cheese, and garlic-chili croutons **123**
Filled polenta cannoli with salted cod and carpaccio **55**
Fish risotto from Burano **74**
Fregula with bevarasse clams **178**

G

Grilled eel **141**
Grilled squid with squid ink and black sauce **136**

H

Herb crêpes with rosemary ice cream **208**

K

King & Queen risotto **194**

L

Liver alla Veneziana **158**

M

Mezzi paccheri with raw fish and tomato sauce **30**

O

Octopus salad **218**

P

Pan-fried artichokes in an artichoke waffle **54**
Pan-seared tuna tagliata with purple artichokes **100**
Puffed red lentil maccheroni with mullet busara **110**

R

Risotto à la Hemingway **22**
Risotto Cotto & Crudo **58**
Risotto with market-fresh vegetables **182**
Risotto with smoked eel, Botìro di Primiero (alpine butter), Castelmagno, and lime gel **40**

S

Saffron-infused sardines in sour marinade **218**
Sautéed clams and mussels **84**
Scampi in white wine **217**
Spaghetti Aglio e Olio with mussels, lime, and Crusco pepper **150**
Spaghetti with crab claws and zucchini blossoms **200**
Spaghetti with seafood **116**
Stockfish mousse spread **72**

T

Tempura-fried zucchini blossoms filled with ricotta and basil pesto **46**
Tuna meatballs **218**

V

Venetian-style fried doughnuts **157**

W

Wellington-style sea bass with oyster sauce **196**
Wild sea bass with garlic, oil, chili, sautéed spinach, and celery purée **36**
Wild sea bass fillet with lime sauce, mashed potatoes, and salicornia **48**

Z

Zabaione **86**
Zucchini blossoms with stockfish **218**

IMPRINT

CALLWEY1884

© 2025 CALLWEY GMBH
KLENZESTRASSE 36
80469 MÜNCHEN
buch@callwey.de
+49 89 8905080-0
www.callwey.de

Find us on Instagram:
www.instagram.com/callwey

ISBN 978-3-7667-2833-3
1st Edition 2025

BIBLIOGRAPHIC INFORMATION OF THE GERMAN NATIONAL LIBRARY
The German National Library records this publication in the German National Bibliography. Detailed bibliographic data can be accessed online at <http://dnb.d-nb.de>.

WE HOPE YOU ENJOY THIS BOOK WITH BEST WISHES FROM:
Author: Christine Countess von der Pahlen
Project Manager: Anna Seidel
Photographer: Mayk Wendt
Editing: Sabine Wölfel
Final Proofreading: Asta Machat
Design & Layout: Sina Preuße
Production: Oliver Meier

THE AUTHOR:
Christine Countess von der Pahlen is a well-known name in German travel journalism. Over the years, she has traveled to more than 100 countries and was closely associated with MADAME magazine for 30 years. Her absolute favorite remains Italy – its unique cultural landscape, cuisine, language, Venice, the island of Stromboli, and above all, the joy of life of its people. Discover more about her travels in her online magazine at www.mywonderfulworld.de

THE PHOTOGRAPHER:
Mayk Wendt works as a freelance photographer worldwide, and his work has been featured in numerous exhibitions. He is also a member of the Freelens photojournalist association and the Swiss Professional Photographers Association (SBF).

Christine Countess von der Pahlen: p.19 Ponte Giustinian, p.62 Isola San Giorgio Maggiore, p.63 Bel Sito, p.106/107 Rialto Bridge, p.126 Atombi, p.127 Pièterre, p.142 Palazzo Mocenigo, p.166 La Toletta, p.167 Caffè Rosso, p.186 Giudecca, p.187 Campo Santa Margherita, p.211 Murano Glass Art, p.220 All'Arco, p.228 Gondola Ride